Practical Strategies for Library Managers

JOAN GIESECKE

AMERICAN LIBRARY ASSOCIATION

Chicago and London   2001

While extensive effort has gone into ensuring the reliability of information appearing in this book, the publisher makes no warranty, express or implied, on the accuracy or reliability of the information, and does not assume and hereby disclaims any liability to any person for any loss or damage caused by errors or omissions in this publication.

Cover and text design by Dianne M. Rooney

Composition by ALA Editions in Caxton Light and Novarese using QuarkXpress 4.11 for Macintosh

Printed on 50-pound white offset, a pH-neutral stock, and bound in 10-point cover stock by McNaughton & Gunn

The paper used in this publication meets the minimum requirements of American National Standard for Information Sciences—Permanence of Paper for Printed Library Materials, ANSI Z39.48-1992. ∞

Library of Congress Cataloging-in-Publication Data
Giesecke, Joan.
    Practical strategies for library managers / Joan Giesecke.
      p. cm.
    Includes bibliographical references and index.
    ISBN 0-8389-0793-8 (alk. paper)
    1. Library administration—United States. 2. Library personnel management—United States. I. Title.

Z678 .G54 2000
025.1—dc21   00-057599

Printed in the United States of America.

05   04   03   02   5   4   3   2

Contents

Contents

Figures

Preface

Are you feeling caught in the middle? Do you feel you have many responsibilities? Do you feel that you have to answer to everyone? Do today's top managers seem determined to eliminate your level of the organization? If you are feeling overwhelmed as a manager or department head, you are not alone. Your colleagues are likely to be just as frustrated and concerned.

But don't despair. Today's middle managers are crucial for holding the organization together. This group helps tie frontline staff to top management. You provide the working leadership for the organization, helping to translate the overall organizational vision into the work of the department, unit, or team. You help link your group to the other units in the organization. For today's middle manager, the challenge is not in finding a meaningful position in the organization. Rather, the challenge is to develop practical strategies you can use to help your unit achieve its goals while helping the organization reach its vision.

Most management books address the needs of top managers and leaders. Few books examine the complex role of the middle manager. But this book is designed to help you in your management role. It outlines strategies you can use to successfully manage your unit whether you are called a department head, team leader, or unit head. The first two chapters provide an overview of the changing world of today's managers. Chapter 3 outlines the many new roles you will play in the organization. These include:

Leadership role

Facilitator role

Working leader role

Catalyst role

In chapter 4, you will learn how to succeed as a new department team leader or unit head. Taking charge of a new department or unit requires careful planning and cannot be left to chance. How you begin your job will greatly affect how well you are accepted by your team or unit.

The next four chapters concentrate on the management skills you will need as a manager. While first line supervisors spend much of their time coordinating work and handling interpersonal relationships, managers must add mentoring, planning, and decision-making skills to their repertoire. Of course, good communication skills are essential and middle managers need to ensure that they continually improve their skills in this area.

Finally, chapter 9 describes various ways to organize the department while chapter 10 helps tie the various strategies together for you.

Being a middle manager is a challenging and rewarding experience. This book will provide you with various practical strategies and skill sets you can use to make your position successful and enjoyable.

I wish to acknowledge the help of my colleagues and my office in putting this book together. We hope that both managers and mentors will find these strategies useful.

1

On Becoming a Manager

Get up to speed quickly. Reorient the organization. Produce results in a short time frame. Right wrongs. Repair damage. Restructure. Refocus. Recharge the organization.

Do these phrases sound like the job description you should have seen when you interviewed for your position as a department head? Is this what the job ad should have said? How can we expect new managers to be leaders while satisfying the multitude of audiences from staff to colleagues to supervisors and still get the job done? Are we asking the impossible of our new leaders?

Perhaps we are if we expect you, as a new department head, to meet the new challenges of today's environment while practicing skills from a previous era. To survive in today's changing world, new department heads must develop a realistic picture of what can and should be done. New managers also need to understand that the tried and true management theories of the past will not be effective today. Command and control models of management are ineffective in a changing environment where professionals, managers, and experienced staff expect to have a true voice in the organization.

The challenge for new managers, then, is that they must meet organizational expectations while learning to define what those expectations can be. Managers need to take charge of their positions, to make the position their own. They need to understand how to coordinate activities, facilitate group processes, communicate, and negotiate.

DILEMMAS OF MANAGEMENT

Department heads face a number of dilemmas. You are expected to control the behavior of the members of the department while simultaneously encouraging staff to grow so that they can meet the challenges of changing technology and new service models. Professional librarians will expect to have a real voice in the management of the department. Managing professionals is a form of managing managers. While many professional librarians may not think of themselves as managers, as professionals they manage their time, manage the delivery of services, and manage resources. From that point of view, as a department head, you are a manager of managers rather than a supervisor of staff.

A second dilemma in today's environment is that as a manager you will need to negotiate with the members of the department to accomplish department goals and objectives. Gone are the days when a department head can simply order staff to complete tasks. Today's employees do not accept this style of management as legitimate.

A third dilemma for you is to depersonalize the leadership process while establishing a trusting relationship with the members of the department. You need to concentrate on what needs to be done and how well members of the department are meeting expectations, rather than trying to be everyone's friend. However, how you view human nature will greatly influence your style. That is, as a manager, you will get what you expect. If you think your staff members are not doing their jobs without a lot of direction, then you will find fault with much of what they do, even if others think the work is fine. If you think people are generally trying to meet expectations, then you will see effort and success, regardless of how well the work is performed. The challenge as a manager is to understand your assumptions and learn how to see beyond your own limited view.

A fourth dilemma you face is that organizational life is both rational and irrational. While some activities can be outlined and will follow standard operating procedures, other events will appear random and chaotic. Management is the art of maintaining direction while managing chaos.

STRATEGIES FOR SUCCESS

A variety of strategies can help you succeed in this new world. A short version of some of the tried and true strategies that can help you get started is listed below.[1] These strategies will be explored in more depth throughout this book.

1. Learn about your role and responsibilities in the department. As obvious as it may seem, it is your responsibility to discover what you need to do as a department chair. Unfortunately, in many organizations, no one is going to tell you what you are supposed to do. You need to discover what your job entails as you learn about the organization.

2. Create a balance between your personal and professional life. While a department head position is very demanding and you will be working long hours, you still need to schedule time for your own personal well-being. You need to find the right balance between advancing in your profession and in your organization and developing a personal life. Taking care of your health, getting plenty of exercise, and taking time to relax are keys to managing a stressful position.

3. Do your own career planning. You should have your own goals for your career. Do you enjoy the management challenges of a department chair position? Are you seeking to advance in the organization? Are you planning to move out of management at some point into a staff position? These types of options are all open to you as you decide how you want your career to develop. By having a plan for yourself, you will be better able to identify opportunities for your advancement and be in a better position to assist the members of your department in their career planning activities.

4. Establish a department vision. As is so often said, "If you don't know where you are going, any road will get you there." As a department head, you cannot afford to allow your department to just drift into the future. You need to help establish a vision and agenda for the department that helps the department move forward as the organization changes.

5. Develop departmental ownership of the vision. Once you have a sense of where the department can go, you need to be sure your department members understand and support that vision. Using participatory processes to create the vision will help department members become involved in supporting the unit's vision, goals, and objectives.

6. Initiate changes slowly. While there are some things that you can change quickly and small problems that may be easy to solve, the process of implementing major changes takes time. Go slowly at first as you learn about the department and the organization. You will design more successful change strategies when you have a better understanding of the unit.

7. Monitor progress toward achieving goals and objectives. Once you have developed a plan with the department for where the department wants to go, it is important to monitor progress and evaluate activities. A plan that is not a living part of the department will not help you and the department remain a vital part of the organization.

8. Allocate resources to achieve your plan. As obvious as it may seem, you should allocate resources to those areas that you want to reward and advance. Too often managers reward bad performance by allocating time and resources to solve problems in areas that are not well run when it may be better to eliminate or change the area or program. Positive rewards will go a long way in helping you achieve your goals.

9. Build trust. Perhaps the most important thing you do as a department head is to create an environment of trust. When the members of the department feel they can trust you and that you trust them, they will be more open and willing to share ideas, opinions, and concerns and help the department succeed.

10. Share information and practice active listening skills. The more information you share, the more the members of the department will come to trust you. The more you practice active listening skills by acknowledging people and summarizing what people say to you, the more they will come to feel that they are valued in the organization. Active listening does not mean you always agree with the members of the department. It does mean, though, that department members recognize that their ideas and concerns have been heard and considered even when these ideas are not implemented.

11. Help your professional librarians and staff set career goals.

Help your department members design career plans and then help them identify opportunities to achieve their goals.

12. Provide feedback on performance more than once a year. People want to know how they are doing at their jobs. If things are going well, they want to be recognized. If problems develop, they will want to know about them before the problems become major concerns. By providing regular feedback to your department members, you can help them develop a sense of how they are doing and what they need to do to succeed.

13. Serve as a role model. You need to practice the same good behaviors and habits you want your department members to practice.

14. Encourage and support your department members. This includes everything from mentoring junior members of the department to providing encouragement and rewards to senior members of the unit.

15. Balance being an advocate for your department and an advocate for the organization. The challenge for you as a department head is to help your department understand that balance.

While this list may seem overwhelming, or that you are supposed to be all things to all people, much of the work of a department head is a matter of balancing competing demands. By having a good understanding of your own career goals, an understanding of what your department members want from their careers, and an understanding of what your department can and needs to do, you will be in a better position to help your department meet its goals.

STARTING YOUR NEW JOB

While you may be anxious about starting a new position, your first challenge is to let go of your previous position. You may be tempted to respond when former colleagues and staff members call you for advice. However, you need to let your successor establish herself or himself in your old job. You can do that best by staying out of your former department's issues and by referring your former colleagues to their new boss or colleague. Your job is to focus on your new organization and to leave your old position behind.

There are a number of things you can do before you start your new job to get ready for the challenges of being a new department head.

First you should gather as much information as you can about the organization and the department. Hopefully, at your interview you asked about the department's goals and objectives. Did you ask your potential boss what issues the person saw for the department? Did you learn about the department's key concerns for the future? Do you have a sense of the scope of your responsibilities? While you can learn the answers to these questions when you begin your position, it is helpful to have some of this information before you begin.

Consult with colleagues in similar positions about how they started their positions. What types of things did they learn in their first few months on the job? What would they have done differently? What advice would they have for a new person in their organization? While each organization is unique and has its own culture, you can use the information you gather from colleagues to help you identify the kinds of issues and concerns you should look for as you begin your new position.

Next, list what pitfalls you anticipate in your new position. Can you let go of your old unit? Can you recognize when you are making assumptions about how the unit should work based on experiences in other organizations rather than acknowledging the unique aspects of the organization's culture? Can you adapt your management style to bring out the strengths of each member of your department rather than imposing your style on them? Are there things that did not go well in your previous position that you can avoid in your new organization?

Asking yourself tough questions about how you view your new position can help you learn what assumptions you are likely to make and how you can avoid falling into these "assumption traps."

As you move through this book you will have a chance to explore different strategies you can use as you take charge of a new department or as you work to improve and change how your department functions.

NOTE

1. John W. Creswell et al., *Academic Chairperson's Handbook* (Lincoln: University of Nebraska Press, 1990), 1-44.

2

The Changing Environment for Middle Managers

Why don't the tried and true rules of management work anymore? Why can't we just maintain the status quo and keep our boss's anxiety level low? Why do we have to change again and unlearn all the basic techniques and rules that were the core of most management courses? Unfortunately, tried and true techniques of command and control no longer work for us. The world does not function as a well-oiled machine where one best way of doing something can be developed and then everyone can just follow that route. Today we need to be more engaged in the process and not just the tasks of management.

What were the safe management rules that were supposed to work no matter what type of department we were running? Our first principle was that we worked with clear goals and a given technology. We assumed there was a master plan and that if each department worked well, then the whole organization would work well. A second rule was that specialized departments such as legal departments, human resources, or finance and business units made important decisions. Even though the actions of these groups might not help the department, we still let them set the direction. A third basic premise was that we are all budget driven, that the budget drives the services and activities of the department. A fourth major strategy was to be as autonomous as possible and to ignore the overall system. The department head concentrated on protecting and advancing the interests of his or her department rather than concentrating on the overall institutional or systems needs. A fifth principle involved delegation. Good managers were those that delegated and managed solely by results. The manager gave the assignments and the staffs did the work. Management was defined as getting work done through others. Finally, we separated people issues from technical issues and contrasted rational thinking with soft people skills. We separated the people from the job at hand and ignored the impact that attitudes toward work had on getting the task done.

While these rules worked well in the early twentieth century, they do not work well in today's changing environment. Today we need to find ways to integrate our activities and work to coordinate actions among departments rather than leaving issues and actions to individual departments. We need to change because, in part, technology has made our work more intertwined. Actions in one part of the library can easily impact activities in another unit. For example, changes in how records are cataloged may impact how public services provide information to users. Changes in public services, such as moving to an electronic reference request system, impact systems use. Top management alone cannot provide all of the coordination that is needed in today's complex work environment; the middle manager has to take on this role too.

Departments do not integrate by magic. Rather, the natural tendency for departments is to move away from other units, to become autonomous or to create their own set of activities. Middle managers have to consciously work to create and maintain working relationships among departments and to overcome the tendency of the system to disintegrate. "Put simply, nothing fits together (or, at least, stays together) without substantial managerial effort."[1] Unfortunately, managers still assume that tasks will neatly work together simply because a rational plan was developed that says the tasks should fit together, that the workflow should be smooth and straightforward. We have downplayed or ignored all the give and take, listening, and negotiation that needs to occur in order to have a smooth-running system.

As a new manager, you have to learn all the intricacies of the system and how all the parts of the organization are related. You can no longer read a departmental manual and know how to do the job. Instead, as a manager you need to see the connections between units, connections with vendors, and connections with customers, clients, or patrons. This is all on-the-job learning. Worse yet, once you have an idea of how the system works, it is likely to change as patron needs change, vendors change methods or programs, and other departments change how they are accomplishing their goals. Learning about the system and seeking interconnections become an ongoing and crucial part of the middle manager's job.

The challenge for managers is to learn to think in horizontal terms when they have been taught to think from a top-down perspective. While the hierarchical relationships are important, the horizontal relationships and connections are what ensure that the work gets done. Coordination is not easy. It must be developed in an environment where technical people continue to use the same problem-solving systems even though our technical environment has changed, and where professionals continue to use the skills they learned years ago in school despite rapid changes in our world.

LEADERSHIP

Why, when we know that we need to coordinate our work and have been discussing systems needs for years, do we still have trouble with the idea of leadership and how to bring leadership into our organizations? What barriers in today's world make leadership so difficult?

Today's environment is greatly influenced by the individualism of the "me generation" of the last few decades. We have changed from a society that valued community goals and shared visions to a society that emphasizes individual achievement over social good. While the activists of the 1960s sought changes in society as a whole, today's citizens often seek what is best for them regardless of the impact on the larger society. Society's heroes are defined by how much money they make rather than by how they help society. As Warren Bennis has noted:

> As eighteenth century America was notable for its free-wheeling adventurers and entrepreneurs, and early twentieth century America

for its scientists and inventors, late twentieth century America has been notable for its bureaucrats and managers. . . . Unlike either our nation's founders or industrial titans, the managers of America's giant corporations and the bureaucrats, elected and appointed, have no gut stake in the enterprise and no vision. More often than not, they are just hired guns, following the money.[2]

In this environment, people are retreating into their electronic worlds, communicating via e-mail, surfing the Internet for friends, living separate lives, and losing any sense of community. People are not trying to make society better nor is society interested in doing better. We are concentrating on our own worlds and ignoring our neighbors. At work, we want to know what the institution will do for us. We are less interested in what we can be doing to advance the overall goals of the institution.

To make progress as we enter the twenty-first century we need to redefine the roles of our managers and leaders. We need to change managers into leaders. Leaders:

1. conquer their ambiguous worlds,
2. bring innovation,
3. develop the organization,
4. inspire trust,
5. take a systems view of the enterprise,
6. look long term,
7. challenge the status quo,
8. do the right things.

Historically managers have:

1. surrendered to their surroundings,
2. maintained the organization,
3. relied on control,
4. taken a short-range, unit-based view,
5. asked how and when,
6. accepted the status quo,
7. done things right.

Now we need to develop managers as leaders and get away from the distinctions that have traditionally separated our organizations into managers and leaders. But as we have seen and as will be discussed throughout this book, we need to carefully define leadership, to understand that leadership does not just happen. We need to spend time developing professionals into leader/managers, people who can help the department meet goals and get the work done. Leaders cannot stand above the fray and leave the work to their followers. They must be an active part of the organization, providing a vision and direction while helping each individual do the best work possible.

HIGH PERFORMANCE AND MOTIVATION

As a middle manager, how can you both support the individuals in your department and still ensure that the work gets done? Ironically, managers are finding that high performance causes high motivation, not vice-versa. We are finding that effective working environments are motivating. Effective middle managers create effective environments that result in motivated employees.

Unfortunately, if work problems aren't solved, the result is learned helplessness. If employees feel helpless, they become unmotivated. They yield to fatalism and a why bother attitude. By actively addressing issues and problems and taking the initiative to clear up problems, staff feel empowered.

Managers need to balance stress and change for their departments and employees. We know that moderate stress yields energy and creativity. We find that no stress causes routine dullness.

For there to be motivation, you will need to balance security and insecurity (see figure 2.1).[3]

Solving or working on performance and work problems with employees increases your credibility. As a manager, you need technical knowledge to participate in discussions with subordinates. You can become a proactive boss and act as a buffer for the department. Here you represent the department, take action, and interact for empowerment.

SECURITY	INSECURITY
Comfortable targets	Stretch targets
Clarity of goals	Ambiguity

Figure 2.1   Motivation

To help improve performance, avoid monitoring work as a numbers game or as punishment. Do not be a scorekeeper.[4] Instead, look for anomalies and discontinuities in the data. Review systems first to see where problems are rather than assuming anomalies are indicative of poor performance by individuals.

While senior management may create overall organizational culture,

> Often overlooked is the more local influence of energetic and skillful leaders within middle management. By means of the behavior they model and their willingness to take personal career risks to challenge and sometimes change the external constraints operating on their work systems and subordinates, they can create a unique and highly motivating subculture within a larger organization.[5]

In brief, motivating environments come from managers who are technically proficient and involved.[6] They create exciting work settings that are progressive, oriented toward change, and problem solving. They engage in meaningful give and take with employees. Staff learn that their knowledge is taken seriously and that they can influence decisions. These managers are leaders.

Nonleaders hold tight to routines and procedures and wait for top management to make decisions. In their departments, the work setting is bland and employees learn to be helpless.

TODAY'S ISSUES

In addition to understanding how to create an internal environment that is motivating, you also need to understand the external environment and how it can impact what you are able to do. Today's middle managers cannot afford to rely solely on top management to monitor external forces. Rather, as a manager, you now need to be outward looking, keeping track of the broad issues that impact your department. Some of the key external and internal issues you will be facing include the following:

Quality. A major concern throughout service industries is the problem of ensuring a quality product at a time when we have yet to develop good measures for quality of services. Nonetheless, as a manager you want to strive for excellence in an environment that resists defining excellence. While some staff will argue for perfection as the standard for quality, as a manager, you need to find a balance between quality and available resources, and between quality and quantity of work done. It will not be an easy task.

Diversity. Diversity today is more than just affirmative action programs. It is the whole process of promoting acceptance of and respect for different opinions, ideas, and people.

Funding. As always, resources remain an ongoing concern for any public entity. Making the best use of the resources you have and seeking alternative sources of funds will be a key to success.

Recruitment and retention of librarians and staff. The hiring decisions we make are some of the most important decisions we face. Finding, recruiting, and keeping quality librarians and staff will be a challenge. Hiring mistakes can be costly. Thus, hiring is not a decision to delegate blindly. Work closely with immediate supervisors, with faculty, and with staff to be sure that the best candidates are identified and encouraged to join the department.

Professional development. Ongoing mentoring and professional development are essential. Professional development cannot be seen as an add-on to our work. It must be a core part of what we do to make the organization a success.

Workload issues. Defining how best to divide the workload when work processes and workloads are changing will be another challenge.

Evaluation of performance. Gone are the days when we can ignore the need for a true evaluation of performance. In today's litigious environment, it is important that personnel issues are addressed and that appropriate and accurate documentation is kept.

Ethics. Ethical judgments and actions must be practiced. The professional code of ethics outlines key values for the profession. Institutional policies and procedures can help as we implement ethical values. Without a strong ethical base for decision making, leaders cannot create the environment of respect and trust that is necessary for a department or unit to be successful.

By tracking these kinds of issues and understanding how changes in these areas can impact your department, you will be able to help your department navigate through external and internal changes while staying focused on its goals and objectives. You can help prevent a crisis by anticipating changes in these issue areas and help your unit plan for these changes.

LEGAL ENVIRONMENT

As a manager, you will need to be familiar with a variety of legal issues that are common in today's organizations. As an administrator, you will be working on contractual issues, including personnel matters as well as constitutional concerns such as free expression, due process, and administrative rules and regulations. You should have a basic understanding of key laws that impact your organization, be aware of changes in the legal environment that impact what you can do, have a thorough knowledge of organizational procedures, and be familiar with the type of legal counsel and support you can get from the organization.

Perhaps the most familiar area of the law for you will be laws that affect personnel situations. Many of the employment situations you will encounter are covered by contract law. "A contract involves a set of promises that create a duty of performance under the law and the right to a legal remedy when they are breached."[7]

The employment contract can range from a formal letter of offer or written contract to a detailed collective bargaining agreement. The contract may be supplemented by state statutes and regulations that cover employment issues. In addition to written contracts, institutional customs and policies can be cited to fill in information gaps in an actual contract. As a department head, you are responsible for knowing and carrying out the terms of the employment contract, including understanding how common practice in the unit may be part of an unwritten yet binding agreement.

Hiring Decisions

Numerous laws and regulations guide the hiring process. Employment decisions must be based on the individual's qualifications and not on characteristics that can be considered discriminatory such as race, gender, national origin, age, and so on. Interview questions must focus on the position and the knowledge, skills, and abilities needed to succeed in the job. The search process must be open and fair, giving all qualified applicants an equal opportunity to be considered.

When conducting interviews you must be careful. Not only must you guard against illegal questions but "the emerging tort of negligent hiring holds employers liable for the failure to discover key information about an employee that reasonably might have prevented harm and liability to others from the employee's actions."[8] Be particularly watchful when hiring librarians and staff who will work with children or provide public service. Usually, legal counsel or a human resources department for your organization can help you in designing a search process and interview questions that can identify potential problems and still protect the institution.

Affirmative action programs may also govern how you recruit, hire, and promote people. This area of law is rapidly changing as court cases are redefining what types of programs are legal. Thus, this is an area where you should be well versed in your organizational rules, and closely follow changes as they occur. With affirmative action programs in mind, you will want to be conscious of the need to bring diversity to the organization. As a manager, you will find you need to steer carefully among potentially conflicting regulations.

The Americans with Disabilities Act (ADA) also prohibits discrimination based on a person's disabilities. "The statute requires that institutions ensure equal access to opportunities and services to persons with disabilities by making necessary 'reasonable accommodations' without 'undue hardship' to the institution."[9] The ADA impacts both how you treat your staff and how services are provided to patrons. Service policies need to be reviewed to ensure that disabled patrons have equal access or that an accommodation is made to provide services. For example, in an older library where the bookshelves may be too close together to allow wheelchair access and shelves cannot be spread apart, a reasonable accommodation could be to provide a service to page books for these patrons. In deciding how to provide an accommodation, it is important to work with the organization's legal counsel or ADA compliance officers to be sure you are providing a reasonable, legal accommodation and not creating an undue hardship for the organization.

This section has touched on only a few key legal issues that impact your position as a department head. As you become familiar with your organization, you will want to develop a good working relationship with the organization's legal counsel and other support units so that you can get advice as you need it to navigate through today's complex legal environment.

CONCLUSION

In today's world, the traditional management theories that stressed stability and control no longer explain how to have a successful organization. Instead of concentrating on controlling activities within the unit, today's department heads must learn how to integrate their units with other departments in their organizations while monitoring external and internal forces for change. The successful manager will be the leader who can take a systems view of the organization and can create the connections between units and between the unit and the environment so that the organization as a whole can succeed.

NOTES

1. Leonard Sayles, *The Working Leader* (New York: Free Press, 1993), 51.
2. Warren Bennis, *Managing People Is Like Herding Cats* (Provo, Utah: Executive Excellence Publishing, 1999), 31.
3. Sayles, *The Working Leader,* 115.
4. Ibid., 123.
5. Ibid., 128.
6. Ibid., 129.
7. J. Douglas Toma and Richard L. Palm, "The Academic Administrator and the Law, What Every Dean and Department Chair Needs to Know," *ASHE-ERIC Higher Education Report,* vol. 26, no. 5 (Washington, D.C.: George Washington University, Graduate School of Education and Human Development, 1999), 6.
8. Ibid., 54.
9. Ibid., 34.

3

New Roles for
Middle Managers

By now you may be asking yourself, "Exactly what is a middle manager today?" What roles will you be expected to play in the organization? Are you a leader/manager or a manager/leader? Are you a team leader, a coach, or a facilitator? Are you supposed to be everyone's friend or no one's friend?

The simple answer to these questions is you are all of the above. But that is not likely to be helpful advice. How can you do all these things and still survive? More importantly, how can you do much of anything when you will be spending close to 70 percent of your time in meetings?

Part of today's challenge for managers is to first understand the different roles that are needed in the organization. Then the manager needs to learn how one can fulfill those roles. Finally, you will come to learn how to use all that meeting time effectively so that meetings become a vehicle for accomplishing your goals instead of being a drain on your time.

LEADERSHIP ROLE

Leadership is one of the key roles for middle managers. It is time to move past the traditional view that leadership is the sole responsibility of top management and to recognize that leadership must exist throughout the organization. The old adage that leaders provide vision and managers implement that vision and maintain the status quo simply will not help you succeed today. Instead, as a manager, you must bring leadership to your department and share it throughout the organization.

What do we mean by leadership? While we may not be able to define it, we can describe leadership. Leadership is doing the right things by understanding the mission, having a vision, and helping the organization move toward the vision. Leadership creates a "social structure of the organization that is capable of generating intellectual capital."[1]

Intellectual capital is the ideas, innovations, learning, and know-how that make it possible for our organization to change and succeed. Our staffs want leaders who provide a purpose for the work, who are trustworthy, who are optimistic about the future, and who get results. They look to their leaders to communicate the vision for the unit, to be reliable, and to know their own skills. Good leaders have a realistic sense of their own abilities and understand that they need to compensate for their weaknesses while capitalizing on their own strengths.

When leadership is effective, the people in the unit feel valued and empowered. They understand that learning is important and will be rewarded. A sense of community is formed as people understand the goals of the unit and how they can contribute to those goals. Finally, when good leadership is practiced, work becomes exciting, fascinating, and, hopefully, fun.

In today's postbureaucratic organizations, we need leadership that is "interactional, that encourages healthy conflict, that is more concerned with cross-functional education and training, that rewards good coaches, and that promotes people who listen to the ideas of others, who abandon their own egos to the talents of others."[2]

Leadership is a creative enterprise: leaders create exciting organizations and promote creativity by others. To create exciting, successful organizations, leaders

1. need to have a compelling vision,
2. create a climate of trust,
3. create meaning for the unit,
4. learn from mistakes,
5. create flat, flexible, adaptive systems.

In contrast, leaders can kill creativity by emphasizing management instead of pioneering efforts, by insisting on harmony at the expense of honest feedback, and by rewarding destructive behavior.

What traits do we look for in today's leaders? Warren Bennis outlines ten characteristics of today's dynamic leader:[3]

1. *Self-knowledge.* Today's leaders need to understand their own skill levels.
2. *Open to feedback.* Leaders need to be open to hearing both good and bad news and to listen to those with whom they agree and those with opposing ideas.
3. *Eager to learn and improve.* Leaders cannot sit back and observe the organization from afar. They need to be active participants, asking questions, listening to others, and always open to learning about the organization.
4. *Curious, risk-takers.* Leaders must be willing to try new things and to learn from the experience.
5. *Concentrate at work.* Leadership is not passive. Leaders have to be engaged in the organization.
6. *Learn from adversity.* We learn more from mistakes and miscues than from successes. Good leaders look to problems as opportunities for learning.
7. *Balance tradition and change.* Perhaps the hardest thing for new leaders to do is to slow down enough to understand the culture of the organization but not become so trapped by tradition that they cannot implement changes.
8. *Open style.* Leaders need to be open to new ideas and open to learning from their experiences. They must be reflective, thinking about how they can improve based on feedback and learning.
9. *Work well with systems.* Leaders must understand the different parts of the organization and how to ensure that work is assigned to the appropriate area within the organization. In

other words, leaders cannot "do it all themselves." They must rely on the systems in the organization to accomplish tasks and projects.

10. *Serve as model and mentor.* Leaders help grow new leaders. Mentoring others, serving as a role model, and encouraging the development of leaders throughout the organization are a key responsibility of today's leaders.

FACILITATOR ROLE

The facilitator role may be the least understood role for today's department chair, as management classes concentrate on leadership and management rather than facilitation. In the facilitator role, you are concerned with helping people to do things, helping your staff or group get their tasks done and meet established deadlines. The facilitator is most concerned with the process the group is using to accomplish tasks, with helping people understand the shared vision and common mission for the group, and with helping the group understand the meaning and purpose of what they do.

Notice that the facilitator role is a helping role. You are helping a group do its work and you have to trust and support the outcome the group creates. You have to let the group take responsibility for its tasks and not step in and try to control the work or the outcome.

You will usually use the facilitator role when you are working with a group. Your primary focus is to help the group complete its tasks. To succeed as a facilitator, you will need to engage the group in the process of getting the work done. To help the group work, you need to be flexible in your approach to meetings and know a variety of techniques to ensure good group processes.

The facilitator role is particularly useful when you need the group to develop a strong sense of commitment to completing a task. By encouraging group participation in the process of getting the work done, you are more likely to build support for and commitment to the task and outcome.

Effective Meetings

There are many resources to help you work effectively as a facilitator with the group.

First, knowing how to run an effective meeting is crucial for the facilitator/manager. Meetings can be a very helpful way to share information, solve problems, gain cooperation for a project, generate ideas, promote team spirit, or provide training or explain new techniques. Good meetings can help encourage camaraderie, improve group processes, enhance communication, or enable people to share values. Poorly run meetings can destroy camaraderie, upset group processes, complicate communication processes, or lower morale for the group. As a department chair you will spend over 70 percent of your time in meetings. Poorly run meetings will waste both your time and the time of your staff.

Effective meetings are those with a clear purpose and a well-planned agenda. First, clarify the purpose of the meeting. Some meetings may be for problem solving; some may be for sharing information; some are for making decisions. Participants should be clear about the purpose of the meeting so that they can come prepared to share information and participate in problem-solving efforts. Once the purpose of the meeting has been clarified, the agenda can be developed. The agenda should list the topics to be covered in the meeting and the amount of time allocated to each item. It is important not to overload the agenda so that each item can be adequately discussed. Putting too many items on the agenda will mean that the topics will not receive the attention they need. This can result in hasty decision making, poor problem-solving efforts, or inadequate sharing of information. Participants can become frustrated by the meeting and less willing to participate in future meetings. The agenda should also indicate who is responsible for each item so that participants will be prepared for the meeting.

In addition to ensuring a workable agenda, a good facilitator will pay attention to the physical environment for the meeting. Room arrangement can greatly impact how communication occurs within the meeting. A formal setting will result in one tone, while an informal setting will result in another. Lighting, temperature, type of chairs, and refreshments also impact the setting for the meeting. A well-ventilated, well-lighted room with minimal distractions can help ensure a successful meeting.

A well-planned meeting can still be a failure if the meeting itself is not well run. Keeping to the agenda, keeping the conversation focused, and keeping the tone of the meeting positive will help ensure success.

Summarizing the discussions as they occur and reviewing conclusions reached will help keep the meeting on track. Keeping minutes is also important so that decisions reached during the meeting will be recorded and remembered. Minutes should indicate not only what decisions were reached but also should state who is responsible for implementing those decisions. Summarizing the end of the meeting and ensuring that all decisions are appropriately recorded are a good way to wrap up the meeting and make sure that participants know what the outcomes of the meeting are. Subsequent group meetings can be used to outline progress on decisions and record the follow-up actions that have occurred between meetings.

Well-planned meetings can then be an effective way to promote group processes, to accomplish group tasks, and to encourage the sharing of ideas among participants.

Tools for Facilitators

Second, you will need a variety of techniques or tools to promote group processes. In *Managers as Facilitators,* the authors describe a number of tools you can use. These include techniques such as "brainstorming, affinity diagram, cause and effect diagram, force field analysis, and debriefing."[4]

Each of these can be useful when used appropriately. For new department chairs, the challenge will be to learn to be comfortable with a variety of techniques and not assume that one technique can be used in all circumstances. For example, brainstorming may be a way to get a group to generate ideas, but is not necessarily helpful when the group needs to focus its energies and make decisions. Nor is it a useful way to set a meeting time or choose a secretary. Process mapping is a way to help a group develop a step-by-step work process or procedure, while cause-and-effect diagrams help organize information about a problem. Affinity diagrams help in organizing a long list of ideas, and multivoting can help a group then choose among the ideas. Finally, debriefing can help the group evaluate a task or experience.

The key for you as a facilitator is to be willing to change techniques or use different tools if the group has become stuck or is not responding or working well.

You need to be comfortable moving between roles, serving as a facilitator when you want to help the group process, and moving to a leadership role or working leader role as needed. Not every decision has to be made in a group process. Instead, learn when the group process is the key to a successful outcome and use the facilitator role to help the group work through its process issues to accomplish its tasks.

FROM MANAGER TO WORKING LEADER

How can a manager move to coordination instead of staying with the tried and true system of separation? First, you need to remember that management requires working leaders who understand the work of the unit and of the organization. You need the ability to keep adapting, modifying, changing, and rearranging complex tasks and functions to respond to changes in the system. You need to look for places where the system is out of alignment and make adjustments in coordination with other departments. If you do not intervene in the system, the forces that create interdepartmental arguments and interpersonal conflicts will prevail.

Another aspect of coordination is to recognize that people and technical issues are intertwined, as are technical and business issues. Technology cannot be separated from what we do and how we do it. The solution to a technical problem needs to take into account the impact the solution has on the people who are using the technology and have to implement it. Coordination issues need to be addressed as technical solutions are being proposed. People issues also cannot be separated from the work. In today's world, staff members must be able to work well together. There are few, if any, jobs left in our institutions where one can work alone. People have to be able to interact well to accomplish common goals.

Coordination also involves managing upward in the organization. Here you need to build support for new ideas or changes that need to occur to promote coordination. Without upper management's support, it becomes even more difficult to effect a change in the overall system and to promote interdepartmental cooperation and coordination.

Good peer relationships are also crucial to cooperation. Credibility is a key. As a manager, you need to know enough about the overall operations to discuss options with other department heads. You cannot bluff your way through these negotiations but rather, you must have a good understanding of the system. You also need to be seen as responsive to others and willing to accommodate others' needs. Peer negotiations will break down quickly if you assume everything has to go your way and only your way.

Within the department you need to think about delegation differently. Traditionally, delegation has been deciding who should do a task, telling the person about the task that needs to be done, checking that the task is being done, and verifying that the task is accomplished. Decision making by the employee is limited in this process. In an environment of working leadership, delegation needs to be an interactive process that recognizes the expertise of the employee, maintains employee motivation, and still keeps the manager involved in the department. Balancing these needs is the challenge to today's manager. In interactive delegation:[5]

1. You need to have the technical knowledge to contribute to the problem solution process.

2. Solutions come from discussion with the staff in a joint problem-solving mode. Participation isn't just a motivational ploy. It is the key to developing rich, appropriate solutions to complex problems.

3. As the manager you bring broad contacts and knowledge of the institution to the problem-solving process. The staff brings creativity and initiative to the process.

4. The process can occur at any time. Meetings are not essential to have good problem-solving discussions.

5. The process brings you closer to the staff and helps decrease the gulf that can exist between employees and management.

6. You are in a position to influence the overall implementation process and to convince other departments and units to consider the ideas of your unit. Building partnerships will be a key to successful implementation.

7. Finally, delegation is not micromanagement. Interactive delegation is a dynamic process that involves you and your staff in a joint process. In micromanaging, you take the decision-making responsibility away from your staff. In interactive delegation, everyone is part of the decision-making process.

In reviewing decision-making processes, working leaders become adept at balancing and molding contradictory requirements. The balancing act may make you feel like a hypocrite as you appear to be inconsistent in your behavior. For example, you will find that you:[6]

1. Practice delegation but get involved in the work,

2. See the big picture but deal with a great many details when resolving problems,
3. Try not to overanalyze a situation while deciding when to jump in and try something new,
4. Respect the formal organizational structure and rules and policies while, at times, making decisions that bypass those same rules,
5. Be conscious of the need to make timely decisions and still be reflective when needed,
6. Stand firm on some decisions while compromising on others,
7. Be loyal to the boss's directions while openly challenging some decisions or strategies.

While decision-making strategies are covered in more detail in subsequent chapters for the working leader role, you need to become comfortable with the ambiguity of acting while ensuring and encouraging members of your unit to take responsibility and be accountable for their own actions and decisions. By promoting broad participation in the decision-making process, you can be reassured that sensible trade-offs are more likely to be made and that the decisions that are negotiated can then be implemented.

MANAGERS AS CATALYSTS

The final role for department heads is that of the catalyst. As a manager, you cannot make an employee productive.[7] Instead, you are the catalyst that can speed up the interaction between employee talent and the needs of the company. You help employees meet goals and plan their careers. Still, success requires a lot of effort by the employee. While you can guide employees toward success, they will succeed mainly because of their own efforts.

You can, however, design systems that help to develop excellence in your staff.[8] First, focus on outcomes and then let employees find the best way to meet those outcomes. Next, value excellence in all positions. This includes every position in your unit, including clerical positions. Celebrate personal achievement whether from the top professional in your area or from the custodial staff. Third, study the best people in a particular position and learn what makes their work excellent. Look for strengths and successes rather than analyzing failures. Then share this information with your group. Finally, in the catalyst role, you motivate people by focusing on strengths.[9] Find out people's strengths, weaknesses, goals, and dreams. Then emphasize their strengths. Treat people as they want to be treated, not as you want to be treated. That way you will be providing them with what they need to succeed. Spend time with your best people and help them feel valued.

Unfortunately, as department chairs and managers, we often find ourselves spending all our time addressing problem employees. Instead, minimize the impact that the problem staff have on your unit, give them less of your time, and spend your time and effort on your best people. You need to address problem staff and problem employees, but don't let that be your only focus. Remember and reward excellence on your staff if you want to promote excellence.

Finally, find the right fit or job for each person. Help your staff with career planning and development. Don't overpromote. Instead, help people identify goals that match their talents. Provide a safety net for people as they try new things. Help your staff stretch their skills; then reward people for trying. Never punish people for trying new things, particularly when you have encouraged them to do so.

One temptation when developing systems to promote excellence is to then try to create perfection.[10] Perfection assumes there is one way to do things and that it (the only way) can be taught. Unfortunately, a system that assumes there is only one way to do things will kill creativity, independence, and learning. Instead of trying to bring conformity to the group, enjoy the diversity of talents and do not try to perfect people.

As a department chair, you may also try to establish one way to do things if you assume people can't do the job. Then you'll put in controls. But, ask yourself, "Why did I hire someone if he or she did not have the talent for the job?" Instead, hire for talent, train for skills, and encourage creativity. Then you can strive for excellence. Another idea that does not fit with your catalyst role is that trust must be earned. This too is a way to enforce controls and leads to mistrust and nagging. Trust your staff to do their best and they are more likely to try to meet your expectations.

Finally, define outcomes in terms of what's right for your customers, your company, and the individual employee. While not all activities have quantifiable outcomes, do try to define what is expected rather than defining how to accomplish the task.

FOCUSING THE DIFFERENT ROLES

Another way to look at the different roles you play as a department chair or manager is to look at how you will focus your efforts at managing the unit. There are three distinct areas that are all part of your position: managing systems, managing people, and managing work. "A systems focus is primarily conceptual; a focus on people is primarily personal, interpersonal, and interactive; and a focus on work is primarily action oriented."[11]

Managing systems is the process of looking at the big picture and finding connections among the many parts of the unit and the organization. In managing systems you are trying to understand why things are important to the organization. Managing people includes basic supervisory tasks such as conducting orientations, providing training, completing performance evaluations, as well as examining the issues of cultural diversity, understanding corporate culture, and learning how to best recognize and reward members of the unit. Managing the work is the process of ensuring that the day-to-day tasks of the unit are completed. It includes looking at short-term as well as long-term projects for the unit and ensuring that these tasks are accomplished as efficiently as possible.

As a manager/leader you create quality in these three areas by creating order, inspiring action, and improving performance. Creating order helps the unit see through the chaos of the environment and develop plans of action and processes for carrying out the work. Inspiring action helps people see that they are making a commitment to a worthwhile activity. Improving performance is the ongoing process of looking for ways to bring learning into the organization so that the members of the unit continue to grow and change to meet the changing needs of customers.

In managing systems, you create order by understanding how the systems fit together and by helping the unit design strategies to meet overall goals and objectives. Systems management is the fine art of learning to love ambiguity and chaos while looking for ways to bring order to the day-to-day processes. You can inspire action by helping the members of the unit to see the overall vision for the unit and the organization. This is the art of looking to the future and dreaming of the possibilities that are there rather than seeing only the barriers to progress. The vision for the unit should link the unit to the overall organization and help promote innovations and future growth. Improving performance from a systems viewpoint involves learning how to orchestrate and manage change. This is the process of managing transitions from one state to another, recognizing the turbulence that accompanies any change, and learning how to bring a sense of calm to such an environment.

In managing people, you create order by understanding the differences among the members of your unit and finding ways to bridge those differences. This is the process of encouraging diversity, understanding the consequences of cultural differences, and building a climate that appreciates differences and recognizes individual strengths. You can inspire action from people by creating an environment that encourages development, rewards strong performances, and encourages individuals to achieve personal, professional, and organizational goals. This is your mentoring role that is so important for the future success of your unit. Finally, you can improve performance by working with individuals to enable them to improve skills, learn, and develop.

Managing the work is probably the most familiar aspect of the job. However, even this role is changing. Now, to bring order to the work, you will want to ensure that individuals take responsibility for their performance. You need to be sure that accountability is matched with power and responsibility. In addition, you will want to promote good decision-making skills, ensuring that decisions are made in a timely manner, and addressing barriers to effective decision making and performance. Inspiring action in managing the work involves effective delegation and serving as a guide to others. It means giving up a command and control approach to promote participation and involvement in the design and implementation of the tasks of the unit. Finally, improving performance involves pursuing excellence, instilling pride in creating quality services, and challenging the unit to continually look for ways to reach new standards of excellence.

As a manager, you will find that you cannot focus on all three areas at one time. Rather, you will move between these areas, addressing concerns and questions as they arise. While your focus may change, the underlying values of these roles of creating order, inspiring action, and improving performance will remain constant. These values provide you with a solid foundation for guiding your own work as you work with the individuals in your unit to accomplish goals and objectives.

CONCLUSION

The role of the department chair or middle manager is changing. We have moved from a world where the manager was in control and could dictate what the actions of the group would be to a world where managers spend their time negotiating with others to see that the work is done. You will find that you will have multiple roles. The roles of leader, facilitator, working leader, and catalyst provide you with an outline of the approaches you will need to take to succeed in today's environment. The processes of managing systems, people, and work outline how you can focus your energy and efforts to ensure that the unit is an effective part of the organization. Remembering the values of creating order, inspiring action, and improving performance will help you keep your focus as you move among the different roles you must play.

NOTES

1. Warren Bennis, *Managing People Is Like Herding Cats* (Provo, Utah: Executive Excellence Publishing, 1999), 72.
2. Ibid., 79.
3. Ibid., 89.
4. Richard G. Weaver and John D. Farrell, *Managers as Facilitators* (San Francisco: Berrett-Koehler, 1997), 112.
5. Leonard Sayles, *The Working Leader* (New York: Free Press, 1993), 98-99.
6. Ibid., 155-56.
7. Marcus Buckingham and Curt Coffman, *First Break All the Rules* (New York: Simon & Schuster, 1999), 230.
8. Ibid., 236.
9. Ibid., 141.
10. Ibid., 112.
11. Stuart Wells, *From Sage to Artisan: Nine Roles of the Value-Driven Leader* (Palo Alto, Calif.: Daris-Black, 1997), 12.

4

Taking Charge
of Your
Department

As a new department head, you are expected to
hit the ground running, to assess and evaluate the
department, make changes, and bring about
improvements. However, in your first months on the job, you will
probably feel uncertain and overwhelmed, as you have to learn about
the department while you are keeping the department running. These
feelings of uncertainty and confusion are all part of the process of taking charge.

Taking charge of a department is often described in steps or stages.[1]
While a step-by-step model implies that the process of taking charge is
linear, in reality, the stages or steps may overlap or be revisited as you
work with your department. The process can take up to two years as
you learn about your unit, implement changes, and assess the impact
of those changes. Unfortunately, you may not have two years
to establish yourself as the department head. You will need to establish your leadership of the unit in the early stages so that the unit will
work with you to complete the process of change and improvement
(see figure 4.1).

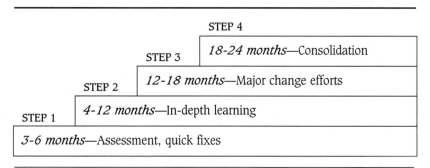

Figure 4.1   Steps to Taking Charge as a Department Head

STAGE 1

The first three to six months on the job is a time of learning and assessment. You need to learn about the department's responsibilities and services, about the budgets and resources available to you, and how the organization itself functions. This is also the time to get to know the members of the department and to assess their strengths and weaknesses.

This stage is also an evaluation stage where you test your assumptions about the organization and the members of your department and begin to assess problems. It is a busy time and one that needs to be carefully thought out. Design orientation sessions to help you gather information and assess assumptions. One of the most difficult tasks in this stage is to keep an open mind and not reach conclusions too quickly. While this is a time to take corrective action, fixing obvious problems or addressing well-understood concerns, it is not a time for major reorganizations or major changes. The challenge is to balance the needs of those who want quick fixes to long-standing problems with your need to learn and understand the organization before making major changes.

STAGE 2

In the second stage, you concentrate on in-depth learning about the department. This period, which can last from four to eleven months, involves little organizational change. It is a time to test the learning from the first few months, refine your understanding of the department and the organization, and assess whether changes made in stage one are successful. It is a time for adjustment and accommodation in which you begin to feel less like a new person and more a part of the organization. The socialization process continues as you move from uncertainty to understanding the organizational environment.

This is also a time when you learn to cope with the ambiguity of the organization and begin to assess what may be feasible. You will begin to recognize more subtle problems in the department and start to find ways to address those deep-seated issues. It is also a time to explore concerns that you identified in stage one but did not have sufficient knowledge to address.

To be successful in the in-depth assessment of the unit, you need to have been successful in your initial evaluation of the department. Again, checking assumptions and clarifying understanding are crucial, as working from inaccurate assumptions will lead to an incorrect analysis of the unit and its problems. The learning in this stage is continuous, diagnostic, and probing in nature. Keeping an open mind now will help you develop a more complete cognitive map of the organization and how you fit within the organization and the department.

STAGE 3

The third stage is again a time for change. Now, with the information you have gathered in the first two stages, you are ready to reshape the department, to introduce major new ideas and efforts, and to address long-standing issues. This stage involves reshaping processes and programs as well as restructuring units. If you have been successful in involving department members in the analysis and assessment of the department, then they will be a part of its change process and can make the process a success. While changes may be announced fairly quickly, implementation of those changes will take time and should be planned carefully to include assessment and evaluation stages.

STAGE 4

Now it's time to consolidate the changes you have made and begin to bring stability to the unit. Learning in this stage involves completing implementation plans and working out any further details in the plans. It is also a time for assessment and identifying follow-through issues that can be addressed in further change efforts.

This stage is also one of negotiation as relationships in the department are realigned to reflect and restructure or process changes that have occurred. As a manager, if you have been successful, you will begin to feel you are truly a part of the department.

ACTIVITIES FOR TAKING CHARGE

Research has shown that successful managers excel at four key areas during their first two years. These are learning, assessment and diagnosis, working out shared expectations, and changing the organization to improve performance.[2]

Learning about the Organization

Successful learning about the organization begins before you start the job. As noted in chapter 1, it is important to ask questions and begin to gather information about the unit and the organization before you begin working. Once you are on the job, you have the opportunity to design a thorough orientation for yourself, meeting with members of the unit, with colleagues and peers, and with your boss. This initial orientation is a time to begin to look for patterns of behavior, spot obvious problems, and begin to identify concerns.

Designing an Orientation

The orientation period is a time for you to learn about the organization. It is your chance to ask lots of questions and to listen carefully to what people tell you about their jobs and about the organization. The data gathering you do during the orientation will serve as the foundation for analyzing the department and for solving problems and designing changes.

In order to keep track of the information, you want to learn about the organization. It helps to make lists of key points you want to be sure to ask and investigate.

In meeting with your boss, you will want to learn:

1. What are the boss's objectives for the department?
2. How do the department's objectives relate to the organization as a whole?
3. What are the expectations for you as a manager?
4. How does the boss want to communicate?
5. What regular meetings are you expected to attend?
6. What types of reports are you expected to submit? (monthly activities, annual reports)
7. What is the budget cycle and when are you expected to submit a budget?
8. What regular activities will you need to cover such as submitting equipment requests or meeting deadlines for materials orders?
9. What is the evaluation cycle, how are you evaluated, what is the process for evaluating members of your department?
10. Are there any agreements with members of the department or promises made to members of the department that you need to know?

Setting up meetings with each member of your department is another important part of your orientation. In meeting with the individual members of the unit, you will want to cover the same set of questions. While the conversations may vary and you may ask additional questions, you will want to be sure you cover the core information. Your staff will likely compare notes after the meetings and if you ask the same questions, they will begin to feel that they are being treated equally. In addition, by asking the same questions, you will assure the members of the department that you are equally interested in each one of them and are not initially seeking information from only a select few members of the unit.

Some of the things you will want to learn from your department members include:

1. What are the person's areas of responsibility?
2. What are the person's top priorities?
3. Does the person have problems or concerns you should know about?
4. What are the person's expectations?

5. How satisfied is the person with the way the department is currently running?
6. What is the workload? Is it reasonable?
7. Are there areas of interest that the person would like to pursue?
8. How satisfied is the person with her current positions?
9. Is the position description up to date?
10. If the person supervises others, does he have concerns about any employees?
11. Do people have the right equipment and skills to do their jobs?
12. What resources is the person responsible for?
13. What other departments does the person work with?
14. Does the person have concerns about other departments or units that as a manager you should be aware of?
15. What is the person's view of the organization's goals and objectives?
16. What are the person's career plans?
17. What changes would the person recommend be considered?
18. What else do you as a manager need to know about the person, the department, or the organization?

By asking these types of questions, you will begin to get a sense of how the members of the department view the department, what changes they would like to see enacted, and how they interact with the rest of the organization. Such information will help you understand your department and begin to analyze how your department works within the organization.

Another important group of people that you will want to meet as part of your orientation program is the other department heads in the organization. The other department heads will be your peers, a group that can be very helpful to you as you learn about the organization. This group can help explain how the organization actually functions, how your unit fits within the organization, and how the units work or don't work together.

Some of the specific things you will want to learn from your peers include:

1. What are their unit's responsibilities?
2. How does the person's department interact with your department?

3. What areas of concern does the person have about your department?
4. What are the strengths of the person's department?
5. What does the person think the strengths of your department are?
6. Does the person have concerns about any members of your department?
7. How would the person like to see the two departments interact?
8. Are there changes the person would like to pursue in thinking about the coordination of activities between the departments?
9. What does the person see as the strengths of the organization?
10. Does the person have any advice about working with your boss?

These kinds of questions will begin to give you a picture of the whole organization and of how the parts of the organization fit together.

When gathering information as part of your orientation program, it is important to keep an open mind and to actively listen. At first it may be difficult to get a sense of the context of some of the remarks you hear. Does the person have an agenda, an ax to grind against the organization, or a personal approach or problem that may be influencing the person's judgment? Is the person really trying to be helpful and honest in his or her responses or is the person not being very helpful? While most people will give you honest answers and try to help you, not everyone will have your best interests at heart. Refrain from making too many judgments based on initial conversations and impressions. This can help you from making mistakes or assumptions.

Assessment and Diagnosis

Beyond the initial orientation, assessment skills are crucial in evaluating the impact of changes made in stages one and three. If the diagnosis of a problem was well done, the changes made are more likely to be effective. If the diagnosis was flawed, the changes may not be working. Then you will need to redesign solutions and try other activities to achieve your goals. As a new manager, you may have difficulty admitting that your ideas are not working. However, letting ineffective efforts continue will do more damage than reassessing the situation and suggesting a different approach. Helping your department understand that change is a constant and that flexibility is a key to success will be more important to your overall success.

Shared Expectations

Another key activity for a new department chair is that of team building or developing shared expectations. Helping a unit come together to work on a shared vision and shared set of expectations is crucial if you are to succeed as a new department head. Successful managers are those who work well with the managers in their unit, developing a team approach so that department issues are addressed from a department-wide perspective rather than an individual manager's viewpoint. Unsuccessful managers tend to work one-on-one with the members of their unit rather than bringing the group together. The unsuccessful department head becomes a lone ranger, trying to solve problems on his or her own and not consulting with the group. Successful managers are seen as being a part of the department, serving as advocates for the unit as well as supporters of the organization.

While you as a new department head are working on team building, the members of the unit are assessing your style and approach. It will be difficult to create a team environment if you are not seen working out in the unit, visiting staff in their offices or work areas, or generally showing interest in the unit's work. For example, if you always call people to your office when you need to see them, you may be perceived as thinking of yourself as more important than the members of the unit. It will be easier to build a team approach if you can explain the vision and expectations for the unit, are seen as approachable and interested in the members of the department, and seek to address group concerns using good group processes.

Changing the Organization

A fourth key area of importance is the process of making changes in the organization. As a new department head, you will want to address problems and make changes to improve the work process. Successful managers carefully consider what changes to make and when to make them. Changes made in the first few months should address obvious problems and are likely to be incremental. Once you are more familiar with the unit and its work, you can set the stage for major changes. Trying to impose major changes before you have completed a thorough assessment of the unit can lead to resistance by the members of the unit and doom the change to failure. Careful negotiation with the members of the unit about changes can ensure a smoother transition and implementation effort.

New managers should try not to become so involved in analysis that changes are not made. It is too easy to spend all of one's time deciding what to change and not take the risk of actually making the changes that are needed. As a new manager, you need to learn to balance analysis and action so that you help the unit move forward and not end up stagnating and missing opportunities for improvement. It is quite possible that you will think you are making changes before you feel completely comfortable. Experience will help you learn when the moment is right for a change and when action is needed. Starting with small changes lets you build experience in lower risk situations so that you can develop a sense of comfort with larger changes and greater risks.

BUILDING WORKING RELATIONSHIPS

Building effective working relationships is another integral part of the process of taking charge. Managers can spend up to 78 percent of their time interacting with others and up to 50 percent of their time with members of their unit.[3] Developing positive working relationships early in the transition process is a key to success. Effective working relationships are built on a number of qualities including mutual expectations, trust, and influence.

Clarify Expectations

Clarifying mutual expectations about performance, priorities, objectives, and standards should be done in the early stages of taking charge. Part of the discussions with employees should include clarifying performance standards and agreeing to goals for the coming year. By negotiating expectations, the new manager can help set the tone for the department and the direction for the unit. For employees, understanding expectations is essential if they are going to be able to carry out the plans developed with the manager.

Expectations must also be relevant for the individual. The goals and objectives of the unit need to be seen as important to the individuals in the department if the members of the department are to work to achieve these objectives. When the goals and objectives are seen as relevant, the members of the unit are more likely to see the manager as having their interests at heart and will be more open to building a good working relationship.

Trust

Developing trust is a core element in any working relationship. Trust takes time to develop. It comes from honesty and reliability. Employees will learn to trust you as a manager when they see that you will stand by your principles, can be relied on to carry through on your word, and are consistent in your behavior. Trust also comes as employees learn your motives for actions. If you are seen as having hidden agendas or being on a witch-hunt, you will not develop a trusting relationship with the members of your department.

Trust is also tied to competence. When you are seen as understanding the business of the unit, of bringing skills to the department, and making sound judgments, trust will develop. While it is important to be informed about the work of the department, it is also important to not get too involved in the details of the operations. The details should be left to the first-line supervisors and the professionals in the unit. They are responsible for carrying out the day-to-day work of the unit.

Trust also comes from clear communication. The more you share information with the unit, and are clear about your priorities and expectations, the more the members of the department can feel confident about working with you and the more trust will develop. Managers in your unit and professionals may have difficulty initially in being honest with you. They may not feel comfortable telling you about problems and concerns. As you explain what you expect from the unit and trust develops, the members of your unit will begin to be more open and honest with you. As that happens, you will be better able to implement needed changes and bring improvements to the unit.

Another key element in building trust is fairness. People in the department need to know where they stand with you. They need to see that you are not playing favorites and are not discriminating for any reason. They need to know that if they meet expectations they will be rewarded. They need to know that the expectations will not arbitrarily change. As the members of the unit see you as predictable and fair, they will come to trust you as the department head.

Developing Influence

A third element in building working relationships is building influence. While you have the authority to make decisions as a manager, your ability to influence the work of others comes as much from your relationship with the people as it does from your position. Influence flows from a number of sources, including expertise, charisma, decisiveness, and willingness to use power. When you are seen to use power effectively to improve the department and when you are seen as an expert in your area, you are more likely to be able to influence the members of your department. Influence then will come from building a good working relationship with your department members.

Good communication skills, conflict resolution skills, and negotiation skills will all help you as you work on clarifying expectations, building trust and influence, and developing positive working relationships within your unit and throughout the organization.

CONCLUSION

The first impression you make with your new department will set the stage for how you and your department will interact. If you carefully plan your approach, design a thorough orientation program for yourself, and keep an open mind as you assess your unit, you can be successful. If you start with a lot of unconfirmed assumptions, assume you know more than the members of the unit, and try to make too many changes too quickly, you will not develop a good working relationship with your unit. By taking your time, assessing the unit and the organization, and balancing action with investigation, you can establish yourself as a manager who cares about the unit and the members of the unit, and can quickly become an integral part of the organization.

NOTES

1. John Gabarro, *The Dynamics of Taking Charge* (Cambridge, Mass.: Harvard Business School Press, 1987).
2. Ibid., 71.
3. Ibid., 99.

5

Mentoring and Managing Professionals

Managing professionals can present a true dilemma for today's manager/leaders. How do you manage, in the traditional sense, professionals or other managers who expect to have the authority and freedom to do their jobs? They are trained as experts in their fields. Why would they want you to manage them? Why would you think you could or should manage them?

Obviously, managing the human resources in your department is not the same as managing the financial and other resources. As noted throughout this book, you cannot expect to control people or issue commands and have people obey you. Instead, you need to think in terms of stewardship, not management. To be a good steward for your department, you want to see the members of your department grow, contribute to the unit and the organization, and reach excellence.

What is excellence? Excellence is delivering the expected results. As you define expectations for staff and the outcomes needed to meet unit and organizational goals, you will define excellence.

Once you have defined what the results are that you expect from your managers and your professionals, you need a way to assess how well they have developed the skills needed to achieve those results. There are five factors that can help you in your efforts to assess your staff. These are: efficiency, effectiveness, employee satisfaction, ability to secure resources, and ability to change or manage change.[1]

1. *Efficiency.* Efficiency is defined as "doing things right." When you are efficient, you are using the finest resources possible to obtain the required results. Efficient units make good use of their resources and produce the desired results for the lowest cost possible. Resources include not only things that cost money, but also time and people's efforts. In an efficient unit, people use time well and accomplish tasks in a way that saves time and money.

2. *Effectiveness.* A second factor is examining whether the manager or professional is "doing the right thing." One can be very efficient and still produce a service no one wants. An effective professional is one who is providing services that your patrons or customers want. "To know whether you are effective, you need to have the humility to ask them."[2]

3. *Employee Satisfaction.* For managers of managers, this is a measure of how well the people in the sub-unit are willing to help and support the manager. For professionals, this is a measure of how well they interact with their clientele. If the people in the unit are motivated and enthusiastic, the unit will perform well. If the clientele is satisfied and working with the professionals in your unit, then the professionals are working well.

4. *Able to Secure Resources.* Good managers and good professionals are able to obtain the resources they need. They can make an effective case for scarce resources, understand the need to negotiate for resources, and be creative in finding ways to obtain or identify additional resources.

5. *Manage Change.* In today's unstable, changing environment, the ability to understand the need to change and the skills to manage change are very important to ensuring success. Good managers and professionals work to bring about change as they work to understand change. Good managers can no longer afford to avoid or resist change. Instead, they need to assess change, embrace it, and then manage it.

USING THESE FACTORS

For each professional in your unit or each manager who reports to you, you need to assess his or her strengths and weaknesses on these factors. Some will be excellent at one or two factors, and good or fair at others. Some will be simply bad at one or more factors. Your challenge will be to help your managers and professionals become good to excellent on all five of these factors so that they will have the skills to meet your expectations for excellence. It is important to remember that you are not seeking perfection and it is unlikely managers will excel in all five areas. Rather, you want to help your managers and professionals become as good as they can in these areas, excel in those that match their talents, and then find ways to help them compensate for areas where they are not as strong. By seeking excellence rather than perfection, you and your staff can set realistic goals.

DEVELOPING PROFESSIONALS

Before you can help the members of your unit develop skills, you should have an idea of how they view the organization. Do they feel they are in an organization that can help them achieve excellence? Marcus Buckingham and Curt Coffman of the Gallup organization have done extensive research on organizations and have found that twelve questions can help you measure the core elements needed to attract and keep the best employees. These questions are:[3]

1. Do I know what is expected of me at work?
2. Do I have the materials and equipment I need to do my work right?
3. At work do I have the opportunity to do what I do best every day?
4. In the last seven days, have I received recognition or praise for good work?
5. Does my supervisor or someone at work seem to care about me as a person?
6. Is there someone at work who encourages my development?
7. At work do my opinions seem to count?
8. Does the mission/purpose of my company make me feel like my work is important?
9. Are my co-workers committed to doing quality work?
10. Do I have a best friend at work?
11. In the last six months, have I talked with someone about my progress?
12. At work, have I had opportunities to learn and grow?

In their study of over 2,500 business units, the authors found that when employees answered "strongly agree" or "5" on a scale of 1 to 5 for these twelve questions, the units were the best by any other measure of success for that industry. In other words, these twelve questions can help you identify excellence and identify the steps you can take to move toward excellence.

The authors also note that the order of the questions is significant. When you first start in your role, you need to know what the expectations are and if you will have the basic resources you will need to meet those expectations. Without these basic elements in place, you will not be able to achieve excellence. Next, you want to know if you can contribute to the organization and if your efforts will be appreciated. Questions three through six will let you know if individuals feel valued for their individual performance and feel valued for themselves as people. By question seven, you can begin to assess whether people feel that they belong in the organization. Questions seven through ten will answer the social questions that are an important part of the environment. Finally questions eleven and twelve measure whether or not employees feel they can grow on the job. To be successful and to want to grow in a position, employees have to feel that there will be opportunities to grow and develop new skills.

Many times in our organizations we begin by looking at opportunities for people to grow without first understanding if they feel they can contribute and that they belong in the organization. This leap in managerial thinking results in our developing organizationwide programs for change without addressing the needs of the individuals in the unit. By beginning with individual needs and ensuring that employees feel they can contribute and feel valued, you will be in a better position to move to unit or organizationwide changes. When individual needs are not met, unit or organizationwide change efforts are unlikely to succeed.

Theories of Motivation

You may notice that the conclusions from Buckingham and Coffman represent something of a change in the way managers have traditionally looked at what factors are important in motivating employees. For example, in the human relations school of management, motivation is tied to job satisfaction and the happiness of the employees. Employees who are happy in their jobs are motivated to do a good job. Two theories of how to improve morale and thereby improve motivation are those of Abraham Maslow and Frederick Herzberg.[4] Abraham Maslow proposed that individuals have a hierarchy of needs. This hierarchy includes five categories:

1. physiological needs
2. security needs
3. affiliation needs
4. self-esteem
5. self-actualization

To Maslow, individuals first need to satisfy their basic needs for food and shelter. Once these basic needs are met, individuals will seek to satisfy their needs for safety. Individuals want to ensure that they will continue to have food, shelter, and a safe environment. Next, individuals will seek to meet their social needs or the need to feel they belong in the unit and are accepted by the other members of the unit. Once the individual feels accepted, he or she will seek recognition for his or her individual efforts. Individuals want to feel useful and appreciated, even in a team-oriented environment. Finally, once all these needs are satisfied, the individual will seek to self-actualize or maximize personal growth. Here the individual seeks to be the best he or she can be in his or her field.

Maslow does note that a person does not need to completely satisfy a need before moving to the next level of the hierarchy. Individuals may partially fill one need while seeking to fill another.

Frederick Herzberg took a slightly different approach to examining human motivation. Herzberg categorized individuals' needs into two groups: those that deal with the environment in which they work and those that determine job satisfaction. In the first group, Herzberg placed five general categories: company policy and administration, supervision, salary, interpersonal relations, and working conditions. These are known as hygiene factors and tend to be dissatifiers. That is, individuals are not motivated positively by these factors, but each factor can have a negative impact on motivation.

In the second group of factors, Herzberg placed recognition, the work itself, responsibility, and advancement. These factors, known as satisfiers, were considered positive motivators. Satisfying these needs leads to positive motivation for the individual and improved work performance.

In today's complex environment, managers are finding that these two theories may not be sufficient to explain what motivates various individuals. Individual needs and wants seem to vary much more than the theorist would have us assume they would. The Gallup studies provide advice on how to look at these theories in today's complex environments. Buckingham and Coffman found that reordering parts of Maslow's hierarchy helped explain excellence. They found that individuals want to satisfy their need for self-esteem (am I contributing to the organization?) before they satisfy their need to belong to the group (do I belong here?). That is, employees focus on individual needs before they become concerned about group processes.

In comparing Herzberg's factors with Buckingham and Coffman's work, one finds that the factors that cause dissatisfaction by individuals are the same. Specifically, Buckingham and Coffman found that individuals most often leave companies because of the supervisor rather than because of other factors such as salary, policies, and so on. Again, Buckingham and Coffman believe that satisfying individual needs comes before looking at group interactions.

As a manager, perhaps the most important point to remember in all of the work on motivating people is that each individual is unique and that a plan that works with one person will not necessarily work with another. It is important that you take time to determine the individual differences and talents that make each person in your unit important to that unit and then design plans that will help individuals improve their strengths and learn to work around their weaknesses.

Individual Plans

Once you have assessed how your employees view the organization and how they view themselves, you can begin to develop plans with them to help them achieve excellence.

There are two important yet simple ways you can begin a professional development effort for your staff. These are monthly individual meetings and monthly unit or group meetings.

INDIVIDUAL MEETINGS

Individual meetings are a key way for you to get to know the members of your unit and to begin working on long-term professional development. These meetings will be failures if you approach them as nothing more than social occasions for a cup of coffee and informal conversation. Instead, these should be formal meetings with an agenda that ensures that you have a chance to listen to concerns and learn about the activities of your managers and professionals. Each month, you should review any personnel issues that may need to be addressed, discuss the activities for the previous month, review plans for the next month, and discuss any general concerns or issues that may arise. While the style or atmosphere of the meeting may be informal or casual, it is important that you cover the key items on the agenda. Your managers have to feel they are being taken seriously, that you care about their concerns and needs, and that you will provide help and support as needed. When done well, these meetings can be an effective tool for keeping informed about your unit while you provide coaching, support, and mentoring to your group.

MONTHLY MEETINGS

While the thought of yet another meeting may not appeal to you, regular visits or department meetings can do wonders for improving communication within the unit and provide opportunities for you and members of the unit to raise issues and concerns.

Here is a chance to discuss common issues and goals, improve coordination among members of the unit and subunits, relay information about organizationwide activities, and discuss unitwide activities. It can also be an opportunity to provide minitraining sessions, introduce new services, or review current procedures. Agendas for the meetings should be distributed in advance, so participants can come prepared to discuss issues or provide input.

While it is tempting to cancel regular meetings when time is short, think twice before you casually cancel this meeting. Canceling department meetings can send a signal to the unit that you do not care about the members of the unit or that you feel your time is too valuable to spend it communicating with them. This is not the impression you want to leave with the members of your unit if you want to succeed as a department head or manager/leader.

Designing Individual Plans

To design a plan to help professionals and managers grow, you need to look at a wide variety of knowledge and skills that today's managers and professionals need to succeed. These include the following:

1. *Knowledge of the global environment.* In today's information world, we all need to understand the global nature of our work. Managers and professionals need to understand both the external factors that impact the global information market and how networked information is changing our worlds.

2. *Knowledge of the organization.* To function effectively in today's complex organization, we have to look beyond our own narrow units to understand how the organization as a whole functions. Systems thinking is a key to survival in our changing world.

3. *Knowledge of the information business.* While the stereotypical librarian may feel that he or she is not part of the crass business world, today's professional has to understand how information resources, multinational corporations, and computer conglomerates are defining our world. We need to understand how our clients' needs are changing.

4. *Basic management skills.* Here you want to ensure that your managers or professionals are practicing basic supervisory and management skills from following procedures for personnel issues to monitoring budgets and ensuring the good use of basic resources.

5. *Planning skills.* Basic planning skills are a foundation for good management. Planning skills include developing projects, meeting budgets, meeting deadlines, following up on plans, and evaluating results.

6. *Interpersonal relationship skills.* Managers must be able to work well with those in the unit as well with others in the organization. Managers have to be able to create and maintain well-run, work-

ing groups or teams. Resolving conflicts, assessing personnel, and creating cooperative units are key indicators of success.

7. *Communication skills.* Management is communication. Leadership is communication. Leaders direct, inform, guide, persuade, reason, inspire, listen, and talk as they influence others. Communication skills can be invaluable when you pay attention to the process of communication and when you remember that nonverbal communication carries more impact than verbal communication.

Besides using good verbal and nonverbal skills to communicate a message, you must also develop skills in getting and giving feedback. Knowing when to listen actively and when to get involved are key issues. When done well, you will be able to learn from your meetings, help people focus ideas, and help them receive constructive feedback without becoming defensive. Good communication skills are a core skill for today's leaders/managers.

8. *Skill at developing others.* While you work on developing managers and professionals in your unit, you will want to see that managers and professionals in the unit are developing others. Assisting junior members of the department, guiding or supporting colleagues, and providing development opportunities for others are signs that managers are becoming coaches and mentors within the unit.

9. *Management abilities.* There are a variety of abilities that today's professionals and managers need to have to be successful. These include analytical abilities, flexibility, adaptability, creativity, ambition, stability, and the ability to multitask (or do more than one thing at a time). Furthermore, managers need to demonstrate integrity, honesty, optimism, enthusiasm, and a sense of humor to survive.

EFFECTIVE DEVELOPMENT

While you may be tempted at this point to simply hand this list of nine factors to the members of your unit and say, "Do this," this approach will not work. Instead, you need to carefully review each category to see how well each person in your unit fulfills or demonstrates these skills. In the areas where the person exhibits strength, you will want to congratulate the person and reinforce the value of these skills. For those areas where a person is not as strong, you will want to develop a strategy with the person for how he or she can improve. While you may feel like throwing all the areas for improvement at the person at one time, resist this approach.

Instead, identify the top priority areas that you feel will have the greatest impact on the person's performance and on the success of the unit and concentrate on those items. Once skills are solid in these areas, move on to lower priority but important items.

By remembering that development is a long-term strategy, you can resist the temptation to implement short-term fixes and instead develop plans that result in long-term and more permanent growth and change.

Coaching

Coaching techniques can help you design long-term strategies for professional development. Coaching strategies include the following techniques:

1. *Events.* These are opportunities to observe the professional or manager in action. Events can be anything from running meetings to conducting a library instruction session to holding a story hour. Your role is to observe the librarian in action so you can jointly critique the librarian's work.

2. *Dress rehearsals.* Here are opportunities to practice a skill or practice for an event. This category can include doing a run-through of a presentation or practicing potentially difficult personnel discussions. The purpose of a dress rehearsal is to give the "actors" or managers a chance to practice a skill and to critique that practice to improve performance.

3. *Delegation.* Effective delegation as outlined in chapter 3 can be an ideal way to coach managers in new skill areas. However, delegation must be well planned to be effective.

4. *Staff assignments.* Sometimes staff assignments can be used to create opportunities for managers to develop new skills or to improve existing skills. Assignments must be meaningful and appropriate. Assignments that are not useful to the organization and do not result in work that is needed by the organization become useless busy work.

5. *Mentoring.* "A mentor is a seasoned professional who takes an active interest in the career development of a younger, less experienced professional."[5]

A mentor serves as teacher, coach, and role model. Why should you be a mentor? A mentor gains psychic rewards as well as tangible benefits from working with younger colleagues. A protégé can help with a project or assignment, freeing the mentor for other projects. A mentor also gains satisfaction from sharing knowledge and skills and helping another professional grow and develop. A positive mentoring relationship can become a lifelong professional friendship.

Being a good mentor requires that you practice good communication skills. Active listening and giving and receiving feedback are key skills. Active listening involves understanding and interpreting what your mentee is saying. It involves understanding what is not being said as well as what is being said as a mentee discusses a concern or issue. Probing in a supportive manner to clarify questions asked can help a mentee learn to focus his or her thoughts, see the broader issues involved in a given situation, and see beyond his or her own point of view.

Feedback, when done well, will help a mentee reflect on an experience, learn from the experience, and begin to formulate ways to build on events and activities.

Each of these strategies can be an effective way to help managers develop and enhance skills. They can work when the participants understand the purpose of the assignment or strategy and participate in the planning and evaluation of the activity. They do not work if the individuals see these as yet more busy work or as efforts on your part to avoid doing your own work.

CONCLUSION

Helping the individuals in your department or unit grow as professionals and as managers is a key responsibility. Career development needs to be a carefully planned activity that involves both you and the professional in deciding how to create opportunities for growth. By working with each member of the unit individually, you can help each member of the unit improve his or her skills and advance in his or her own career. Good planning skills, careful communication, and good coaching skills are the foundation for mentoring your staff members and for designing positive opportunities for growth.

NOTES

1. Harge Franzen and Maurice Hardaker, *How to Manage Managers: A Workbook for Middle Managers* (London: McGraw-Hill, 1994), 54.

2. Ibid., 56.

3. Marcus Buckingham and Curt Coffman, *First Break All the Rules* (New York: Simon & Schuster, 1999), 28.

4. Harold Gortner, *Administration in the Public Sector,* 2nd ed. (New York: Wiley, 1981), 120-23.

5. Rosie Albritton and Thomas Shaughnessy, *Developing Leadership Skills* (Colorado: Libraries Unlimited, 1990), 189.

6
Planning Skills

Coping with constant change has become a standard part of any library manager's position. Successful managers will find ways to cope with and manage change. Unsuccessful managers may feel the best they can do is to move from one crisis to another. These managers never get beyond fighting fires. Rather they become so engrossed in the day-to-day problems that they miss the overall changes that are impacting their departments.

Successful managers use tools that are available to help them manage the change process. One set of such tools is planning techniques and processes.

Planning can be defined as applying rational thought to the future. It is a continuous process rather than a one-time activity. A successful planning process requires managers to devote thought, time, and resources to the activity. Planning done casually and haphazardly will not lead to success.

Planning techniques run the gamut from traditional, planned processes to unplanned change techniques. Each planning process or tool offers managers a different perspective for viewing the environment and coping with change.

TRADITIONAL PLANNING MODEL

The traditional planning model begins with managers identifying the concerns to be addressed. Once the questions are known, the managers develop options for addressing the issues. They then assess those options and choose strategies that help the unit maximize its goals. Traditional long-range plans are often developed using such a process. The technique assumes a stable environment and is most appropriately used when an organization is not facing a lot of changes. Given the changing nature of libraries today and the changing environment, managers will likely find that plans developed using this approach will not be applicable to the organization for more than a very short time period.

ANNUAL PLANNING MODEL

Annual planning processes stress incremental changes. In an annual process, objectives or action steps for the next year are identified and prioritized. Time frames are then attached to the objectives based on the unit's goals and priorities. The time frames establish the order in which objectives will be addressed and completed. At the end of the cycle, progress on objectives is noted, new objectives are developed based on the previous year's results, and the cycle continues.

Annual planning helps an organization work toward its overall goals. Annual plans can be used as a way to implement strategies developed in other planning processes such as strategic planning or scenario planning. The annual plan helps an organization or unit assess progress and make corrections in its overall plans as the environment changes.

STRATEGIC PLANNING

While annual planning processes are useful for identifying incremental changes, strategic planning processes are used to help organizations change future directions in response to a changing environment.

Strategic planning is a disciplined effort to produce fundamental decisions and actions that shape and guide the activities of an organization. It is a disciplined process because it involves a number of steps that are done in a particular order to keep the process focused and on target (see figure 6.1). The decisions that are made in the process will guide the development of the organization and are fundamental to the success of the organization.

---

1. Are you ready to plan
2. Define purpose of the department
3. Complete an environmental scan
4. Develop goals and objectives
5. Develop action steps
6. Implement the plan
7. Assess progress, revise plan

Figure 6.1   Steps for Strategic Planning

Strategic planning is a useful process when it supports strategic thinking and answers the question, "Are we as an organization doing the right things?" Strategic planning is not about making future decisions, nor is it a substitute for leadership and judgment. It is about anticipating the future so that decisions reached in the process will help the organization reach its own desired future.

There are numerous books, articles, and Web sites that describe strategic planning in detail. The key steps in strategic planning are described below, so that managers can determine if this planning tool is appropriate to their situation.

Step 1

The first step in the strategic planning process is to get ready for planning. Here you as the unit manager must assess if the group is ready for a planning process. Answering the following questions will help you decide if your unit is ready to embark on a planning process or if you need to do more preparation before beginning to plan.

Are you, as a manager, committed to the process?

Can you see the "big picture" and help your department understand how the department fits within the total organization?

Do you know what questions or issues you want addressed in the process?

Can you clarify the roles of the participants in the process?

Do you have staff who are willing to be part of a planning committee, or will the department as a whole participate in the planning process?

Can you develop a profile of your unit to show how your unit fits within the organization and the unit?

Can you identify the information that is needed to help in decision making?

If you can answer yes to the above questions, you and your unit are ready to begin strategic planning.

Step 2

Step 2 in the process is to develop a mission statement for the department or organization. A mission statement has three parts: purpose, business, and values. The purpose outlines why the department exists. The business of the organization is the main activity of the department or unit. Finally, values are the principles or beliefs that guide the organization.

The unit also needs to develop a vision statement. While the mission statement describes what an organization is, the vision statement describes where an organization wants to be. The vision statement describes what success will be for the unit. The mission and vision statements help the participants in the planning process understand how the organization wants to develop and grow.

Step 3

Step 3 in the process is to complete an environmental scan or analysis. Once the mission and vision statements are developed, the group needs to assess the current situation or environment for the unit. Here the group identifies the strengths and weaknesses of the department or organization. Then the group describes the opportunities for the department, and the threats or challenges that can keep the department from reaching its goals.

From the lists of strengths, weaknesses, opportunities, and threats (SWOT analysis), the group identifies the top five to ten critical issues that will impact the organization and that will need to be considered in the planning process.

Step 4

In step 4 the group begins to develop goals, objectives, and strategies. Here the group faces the main part of the planning process. In this step the group begins to decide what to do about the critical issues they identified in step 3 in relation to the mission and vision developed in step 2. Goals or what the organization intends to do are outlined. The group outlines strategies or broad approaches to use in addressing the goals. Participants then create objectives or action items describing how the unit will implement the strategies they have developed. Extensive discussion occurs at this stage of the process as the department decides what activities it will pursue over the next few years (strategies) and what actions the group will take in the next year (objectives).

Step 5

Once the mission and vision statements, goals and objectives are developed, a coherent plan needs to be written to capture the ideas and concepts developed in steps 1 through 4. Once written, the plan should be reviewed regularly and should be a blueprint for future actions. Relegating the written plan to a shelf and ignoring it will negate the positive outcomes that can result from a well-organized and participatory planning process.

Implementing the Plan

During the planning process, managers can take steps to enhance acceptance of the plan and thereby improve the chances that the plan will be implemented. To gain acceptance of the plan, managers should:

1. Involve informal and formal leaders in the process to signal the importance of the plan;

2. Provide training for participants about the process so that participants will work from a common understanding;
3. Invite those who will implement the plan to participate in the planning process;
4. Address the critical and difficult issues in the organization in the process;
5. Specify who will be responsible for implementing the parts of the plan as the plan is developed;
6. Limit the amount of details in the plan or the plan will become outdated before it can be implemented;
7. Balance dreams with reality so the plan inspires action but remains relevant to the changing environment;
8. Continue to review and revise the plan so that it will become a tool for management and not just a report;
9. Incorporate the plan into day-to-day management activities to give the plan a foundation and a purpose;
10. Incorporate an assessment and evaluation process into the plan so the plan remains relevant.

Employing these strategies and following the steps outlined for the strategic planning process will yield a successful strategic plan that can help you and the department move forward in a changing environment.

INTERACTIVE PLANNING

While strategic planning is a mainstay of today's management tools, other planning tools exist to help today's managers cope with change. One such tool is interactive planning, developed by Russell Ackoff.[1] In interactive planning processes, planning becomes the primary management strategy for the department and is woven into the fabric of how the department operates. Interactive planning stresses a systems thinking approach to the planning process. While traditional planning processes look at the parts of an organization in order to understand the whole organization, systems thinking begins by examining the organization as a whole and then explains the behavior of the parts in relation to the whole.

Interactive planning involves three main principles: the participatory principle, the principle of continuity, and the holistic principle.[2] First, participation is the foundation of the planning process. Managers and department members are responsible for developing organizational plans. Second, the process is never-ending. Planning is seen as a part of the day-to-day activities of the department and not as a separate activity or process. Third, the process requires coordination and integration. "No unit can plan effectively if it plans independently of the other departments at the same level."[3]

In interactive planning the unit develops its goals and objectives and then designs activities to meet those objectives. As the unit works on these activities, the members of the unit evaluate progress toward achieving their goals. Decisions on how to proceed are based on how well the activity helps the unit implement its plans.

In interactive planning, the written plan becomes a document that is used continuously by the unit to set the direction for the unit. The plan is not something that is reviewed only once a year. Rather, evaluation of the plan is an ongoing process. The plan is completely integrated into the work of the unit.

SCENARIO PLANNING

In times of continuous change, managers find that standard forecasting techniques, such as strategic planning models, may not provide enough guidance for planning when so little is certain. To complement strategic planning techniques, managers can use scenario-planning processes to bring creativity and intuition to the process of data analysis (see figure 6.2).

---

1. Identify the decision to be addressed
2. Complete an environmental scan
3. Identify driving forces
4. Rank the forces
5. Choose themes for the stories
6. Write stories or scenarios
7. Identify implications of the stories
8. Develop plans to address implications
9. Monitor changes in environment
10. Revise scenarios

Figure 6.2　Steps for Scenario Planning

Scenario planning is a process of developing stories to describe possible futures. The stories or scenarios "go beyond forecasts to communicate vividly the meaning and impact of events in a way that clarifies the message."[4] The stories help managers consider a variety of possible futures and to assess alternative strategies that can be effective in a variety of circumstances.

> Scenario planning avoids the need for single point forecasts by allowing users to explore several alternative futures. To be useful, the scenario plots must hang together like a well-crafted novel, stretch the imagination without going outside the bounds of believability.[5]

Scenario planning is actually a process we use without realizing it. We often create stories or plots of how events might develop. For example, imagine someone driving into your neighborhood, seeing a ball in the road and braking, then looking around. These acts are part of the creation of a story by the driver where the key issue is getting home, the driving force is the ball, the predetermined elements are the knowledge that kids and dogs live nearby and could be playing in the street, and the uncertainty of not knowing if children or dogs are nearby and could run into the street after the ball. Such a series of events summarized as a brief plot of "kids and dogs at play" is how we often look at uncertain situations and make decisions about how to react to the uncertainty. Scenario planning takes an approach we use regularly and uses it to develop a structured process for planning.

As noted above, then, scenario planning is a process for describing possible futures that the organization might face. These scenarios or stories are then used to develop strategies that will increase the chances of success for the organization as it responds to a changing environment. Scenario planning is not a process for predicting the future or developing preferred futures. Rather, the process asks participants to imagine multiple futures and then design plans to respond to changes depending on how the future develops.

The process is a structured one that results in key stories the organization can use to describe possible futures. The steps in the process include:

Identify the decision to be made. Here managers decide what question they wish to address in the planning process. If the question to be addressed is not clearly articulated, the participants will not have the guidance they need to develop useful scenarios.

Identify key forces in the environment. As in strategic planning, participants outline srengths, weaknesses, opportunities, and threats that the department is likely to face.

Identify driving forces. Participants identify those trends and pressures that will have the most impact on the organization or department. Driving forces usually come from one of five categories: social, economic, political, technological, or environmental.

Rank the forces. Participants rank the forces to decide which are most important to the department and which are most uncertain. Forces that are certain are ranked below those that are uncertain. For example, in the library field, serial price increases are a certainty. This force is likely to be a factor in any scenario regarding library collections and budgets.

Choose the main themes for developing the scenarios. Here participants look at the interplay of the driving forces and trends to determine what themes emerge. Participants should avoid developing good, bad, and average scenarios. Rather, they need to look for overall ideas and themes that will drive their future. Again, the scenarios are framed by the uncertain and most important forces rather than by the certain, known forces.

Write the scenarios. Here stories are outlined to describe the possible futures. The stories are not complete, detailed descriptions, but rather present the core ideas likely to be seen in the future. The group should develop no more than three or four scenarios. Too many scenarios will unnecessarily complicate the planning process.

Look at the implications of the scenarios. From the stories that have been developed, participants begin to outline strategies that will help the organization respond to changes in the environment. By looking at the implications of the stories, the participants can begin to make decisions about how to respond to change.

Identify ways to monitor change. Participants outline those indicators they will use to review the scenarios to determine if the
future is developing as they described. The indicators help
managers know which strategies might work in response to
the changes the department experiences.

With scenario planning, the manager develops a variety of plans
and strategies so that the department can respond effectively to a
changing, volatile environment.[6]

UNPLANNED CHANGE STRATEGIES

While planning processes can help you manage change, unplanned
change strategies can help you promote creativity in the organization.
In unplanned change strategies, participants act first and then step
back, evaluate the results of their actions, and create a plan. While this
process can bring about an element of chaos, it can also help an organization move forward when the group is unwilling or unable to
change. For example, to develop a marketing plan for the department,
you could ask members of the department to look for opportunities to
market services and then try marketing the service without an overall
plan. The members of the department then evaluate which of the
methods they tried worked and which ones were not as successful.
This information is then used to design a marketing plan for the unit.[7]

While unplanned change strategies can lead to activities that do
not accomplish the unit's goals, unplanned change strategies combined
with planned strategies can help a department or unit respond cre-
atively to a chaotic, uncertain environment.

CONCLUSION

Planning tools help managers respond to changes in the environment
and the organization. By implementing sound planning processes,
managers can move from crisis management to planned responses to
change. Department members can develop a better sense of where the
department is headed and can be a part of the process of making the

future happen. Without planning processes, managers can only respond to change; they cannot help shape that change.

NOTES

1. Russell L. Ackoff, *Creating the Corporate Future* (New York: Wiley, 1981).

2. Ibid., 65.

3. Joan Giesecke and Kent Hendrickson, "Interactive Planning in an Ever-changing Environment" in *Building on the First Century: Proceedings of the Fifth National Conference of the Association of College and Research Libraries,* Cincinnati, Ohio, April 5-8, 1989 (Chicago: American Library Association, 1989), 71-72.

4. Gordon Robbins: "Scenario Planning, A Strategic Alternative," *Public Management* 77 (March 1995): 4.

5. Audrey Schriefer, "Getting the Most out of Scenarios: Advice from the Experts," *Planning Review* 23 (Sept./Oct. 1995): 33.

6. For more information on scenario planning, see Joan Giesecke, *Scenario Planning for Libraries* (Chicago: American Library Association, 1998).

7. For more information on unplanned change strategies used to create a marketing plan, see Joan Giesecke et al., "Marketing without a Plan: Seizing Outreach Opportunities As They Appear," *NLAQ* 21 (summer 1990): 5-10.

7

Decision-Making
Skills

Decision making is the most central function of
management. It is something we do every day,
often without thinking about how we make deci-
sions. But the process used to make a decision has important consequences for the organization. The process affects the outcome, deter-
mines who can participate, what alternatives are considered, and how
a choice is made. Becoming more conscious of the different models you
can use to make decisions can help you make better decisions in your
role as a department manager.[1]

CLASSICAL MODELS OF DECISION MAKING

Most of us have been taught that decision making should be a rational process and rational decision-making models dominate most books
and articles on how to make decisions. Rational decision making is a
step-by-step process. First you identify the problem to be solved. This
is a crucial step, as how you define the problem will impact how the

problem is addressed. Problems can come from anywhere. The problem could be a performance issue, could be one of obtaining resources, or could represent a deviation from a department plan. Part of the process of identifying the problem includes categorizing the problem, identifying the dimensions of the problem, and evaluating the problem. Once the problem is identified, you need to decide how you will evaluate possible solutions. That is, what conditions would exist if the perfect solution were found for the problem? These criteria or conditions are used to evaluate options and solutions.

Next you gather information and generate alternative ways to solve the problem. This is an opportunity for creativity. Brainstorming techniques, nominal group techniques, and so on can be used to help generate ideas for possible solutions to the problem. These alternatives are then ranked in an effort to find the solution that will maximize your goals. The solutions are assessed against the criteria developed in the second step of the decision-making process. In this step you may also want to analyze the consequences of a particular solution so you can thoroughly assess the impact of any particular solution or outcome. Finally, you choose the alternative that maximizes your goals and minimizes your losses, and communicate your decision to those involved in the decision-making process.

The rational decision-making process assumes you have complete knowledge of the alternatives available, understand the consequences of the alternatives, and can choose the one that maximizes your goals. It is a time-consuming process and very information intensive. It works well when the information needed to make a decision is already known or is easy to discover, when there is only one possible decision, when one decision is clearly better than another, or when there is no difference between the costs and benefits of the options. The process is less effective for complex decision processes when information is incomplete and there is a lack of agreement on the problem or the criteria used to assess the outcomes.

ALTERNATIVE MODELS OF DECISION MAKING

Unfortunately for most management situations, you will have neither the time nor the information to follow the rational decision-making process. Instead you will find yourself making decisions with little information and hoping that you find an answer that is good enough. Rather than continuing to try to follow rational processes in an irrational environment, you can learn to use different decision-making systems based on the situation you are in. The key for managers is to learn when to use other decision-making models (see figure 7.1).

Most comparisons of decision-making models continue to view decision making as a series of steps that can be identified and analyzed. The step-by-step analysis makes decision-making processes appear more logical than they actually are. A different way to look at decision-making processes is to examine the characteristics of the organization, the characteristics of the decision-making process, and the methods used to make decisions, and to compare how the different models address these areas.

The characteristics of the organization that are important in looking at decision-making models are:

1. How ambiguous are organizational goals? Does the organization have agreed-to, well-defined goals or are goals ill defined or emerging?
2. How well do participants in the organization understand organizational processes? Do members of the organization know how decisions are made?
3. How structured is the organization? Is there a clear hierarchy? Is the structure less defined, looser, with people behaving independently?
4. How adequate are organizational resources? Does the organization have adequate resources? Are there excess resources so people can take on new projects? Are resources scarce so people are always competing for them?

The characteristics of the decision-making process that are important are:

1. How independent are the participants? Are members of the organization dependent on each other, able to act independently, or are their actions interdependent?
2. How is power distributed in the organization? Is power centralized and controlled? Is it distributed?

VARIABLE	RATIONAL	BUREAUCRATIC	POLITICAL BARGAINING	PARTICIPATION	GARBAGE CAN
Characteristics of Organizations					
Goals	Well-defined	Well-defined	Known, but differ among individuals	Shared, understood	Ill-defined, may change
Degree of certainty	Assumes certainty	Certain	Uncertain	Certain	High degree of uncertainty
Degree of structure	Highly structured	Structured	Unstructured	Structured	Unstructured or partially structured
Adequacy of resources	Assumed adequate	Assumed adequate	Scarce	Assumed adequate	Excess or scarce
Characteristics of the Decision-Making Process					
Degree of independence	Roles are defined	Roles define interdependence	Interdependent	Interdependent	Independent
Diffusion of power	Part of the structure	Defined by the rules	Dispersed	Shared	Dispersed
Use of information	Gathered and used	Rules define use of information	Gathered and used	Shared	Gathered, may or may not be used
Perception of the issue	Important or unimportant	Important or unimportant	Important	Important	Important
Method of solving problems	Value—maximization	Standard operating procedures	Bargaining negotiation	Consensus	Ad hoc

Figure 7.1 Decision-Making Models

3. How do members of the organization use information in the decision-making process? Is information gathered and used or gathered and ignored?
4. How do members of the organization view the issue under discussion? Is the issue important to them, unimportant, or do they simply not care?

You can distinguish among the many decision-making models by looking at the following factors. First, do the individuals involved in the decision-making process share goals, have mixed goals, or keep changing their goals? Next, do those involved in the decision-making process have to work together on a solution or can they act independently? Are there incentives for the individuals to work together to come to a solution? Third, how is power distributed in the organization? If power is distributed, then you will likely need to negotiate a solution. If power is concentrated, you may be able to impose a solution or have a solution imposed upon you. By looking at these factors in the organization, you can begin to distinguish between decision-making models and learn when to choose a particular decision-making approach.

The next sections will outline a variety of decision-making models and explain when each one is most likely to be useful to you.

Bureaucratic Model

One of the more familiar forms of decision making is bureaucratic decision making. In bureaucratic decision making, goals are well defined and the organization has a clear, well-understood structure. Resources may be scarce or abundant. The rules will define how the organization will distribute resources. The rules define who can participate in the decision process and how much discretion participants have in making decisions. Power is not an issue as rules dominate the process. Information will be gathered and used or not gathered depending on the standard operating procedure in place for a given situation. Participants may or may not be concerned about the issue at hand. The organization develops rules and procedures for how routines are to be carried out, and participants then follow standard operating procedures in carrying out their duties. In the bureaucratic model, the rules of the organization define how decisions will be made.

Decisions in such an environment tend to be incremental, allowing for small changes within the organization. While bureaucratic processes and hierarchies allow for coordination of large groups of people in complex organizations, these processes do not encourage or allow for major changes. However, the processes keep the organization functioning in a stable environment and are very helpful for ensuring that routine decisions can be made easily and quickly.

Political Bargaining

Political bargaining decision processes can be very helpful when the organization is made up of diverse interests and multiple goals. In the political bargaining model, the organization is viewed as "alive and screaming political arenas that house a complex variety of individuals and interest groups."[2] Organizations in such an environment have multiple, conflicting goals. Nonetheless, individuals are seen as having consistent goals and purposes. But, because the decision-making process involves multiple participants, participants are not completely sure of how organizational processes work. The organization is structured and the organization's hierarchy and rules determine who can participate in the decision-making process. Resources are considered scarce and it is believed that participants will come into conflict over the distribution of these scarce resources.

In the political bargaining model, members of the organization are viewed as interdependent and it is assumed they will react to the actions of other members of the organization. Power is distributed unevenly in the organization, creating an environment where participants have an incentive to bargain to get what they want. Information is an important part of the bargaining process and will be gathered and used in an effort to increase one's bargaining position in the process. Finally, if issues are important to participants, participants will be inclined to bargain and participate in the decision-making process.

In this type of environment, members of the organization will enter into bargaining situations in an effort to influence goals or outcomes of decision-making processes.

Negotiations and compromises will occur as participants seek to keep the process going long enough to reach a solution. Once participants agree to accept a solution, the process will end. However, the issue may arise again as the losers in the decision-making process may seek other avenues to try to change the agreement to more completely meet their own needs. The individuals will continue to bargain as long as they believe they can influence the outcome of the process. Individuals do not need to agree on goals or values. They only need to agree to bargain.[3]

As a manager, you will find political bargaining models helpful when negotiating agreements with other units or between members of the department who are not in agreement with each other. Here, rational models will not help because the individuals involved in the process are not in agreement about the desired outcome nor will they agree about how alternatives should be ranked. Rather, they will try to maximize their own interests. In such cases, coalition building, compromising, game theory, and bargaining are all processes that can be used to help the individuals reach an agreed-to decision. While the process is messy and may seem irrational, it can be very successful. However, as in bureaucratic decision making, changes are likely to be incremental rather than radical or revolutionary.

Participatory Decision Making

Participatory decision-making processes begin with the assumption that all members of the department have the same goals. The goals are shared when individual needs and organizational needs intersect in a way that allows members of the department to share the department's vision. Participatory processes assume that individuals understand how decisions will be made and accept those processes. Rules are created that help define who can participate in decision-making processes and how those processes will be carried out in a shared goal environment. Resources may be adequate or scarce. However, it is also assumed that individuals will put the needs of the organization above their own needs when there is a conflict. In a participatory process, participants are interdependent and want to work together. Power must be shared or the participatory process will break down and political bargaining behavior will likely occur. Information is gathered as part of the decision-making process and is shared among all participants. There is no reason to use information as a weapon in negotiations in such a shared goal environment. Issues under discussion should be important enough to participants to warrant the time that participatory processes can take. For participatory processes to be successful, individuals in the unit need to believe that keeping the department together and running smoothly are more important than any particular individual interest.

In a participatory environment, many decisions will be the result of the group coming to a consensus on an issue. The members of the department will make a commitment to the decision outcome and will work to keep the group together even if they do not totally agree with the outcome.

Garbage Can Model of Decision Making

One of the more unusual views of the organization is that of the garbage can model. In this model, the organization is viewed as an organized anarchy, with the individuals in the organization seen as independent agents with conflicting goals. Problems, solutions, and people seem to act independent of each other in the organization. Problems appear and disappear without being resolved. Solutions are enacted even when problems have not been identified or analyzed. People appear and disappear throughout a decision-making process, changing the dynamics of the process depending on who shows up for a meeting or discussion. The organization is seen as having multiple, conflicting goals that are not well defined. Individuals can have conflicting goals, change their goals, or be inconsistent in how they look at a given issue. Participants have little understanding of how organizational processes work or how decisions are made. The links between people, problems, and solutions are not always clear and decisions may have little connection to the problem under discussion. The organization is at best loosely structured where rules may or may not help explain who participates in a decision-making process. Resources may be scarce or abundant in this model. When resources are abundant, managers can create enough decision-making opportunities for people to enable individuals to discuss issues without feeling pressure to come to a decision. When resources become scarce, individuals may revert to bargaining behavior to get what they think they want.

In such organizations, people act independently, choosing which decision-making opportunities to attend. Problems, solutions, and people may change even within a single decision-making process. Power is dispersed, with individuals having little ability to influence the overall system. Information may be gathered and used or left unused depending on who decides to remain in the decision-making process. Finally, issues must be seen as important for individuals to spend time on them. Otherwise, people will simply opt out of the decision-making process.

As participants in decision-making processes may or may not choose to participate, the process is fluid and changing. Participants are easily distracted when more interesting opportunities come along. In this environment, decisions are made as much by chance as by design. If all goes well, a decision is made. If anything changes in the process, a decision may or may not be made. While the description of the organization as a garbage can or organized anarchy may seem pathological, it will also feel quite familiar to managers as they negotiate among independent members of their department.

STRATEGIES FOR DECISION MAKING

The challenge for you as a manager is to identify which decision-making model is most likely to apply in any given situation and then to choose the strategy that is most likely to result is a satisfactory decision. For each model, a variety of strategies may be effective, depending on the individuals involved, the outcome desired, and the resources available.

In rational decision making, the strategy for decision making is to maximize goals by choosing the alternative that maximizes efficiency. Unfortunately, except in relatively simple situations, it will be very difficult for you to have enough information and resources to choose the alternative that truly maximizes your goals.

In political bargaining situations, you are trying to achieve a compromise, in which the individuals in the decision-making process are willing to accept the decision because it will satisfy enough of their needs to keep them engaged in the process. Coalition building, compromise efforts, or choosing an alternative that is good enough are all strategies that can be effective in managing the process.

In garbage can processes, you have three basic approaches you can use. You can put controls in the process that will limit when problems can be discussed, limit who can participate in the process, or limit the time available for discussion. Another strategy is to adapt to the process by changing your style to meet the organizational approaches. This can involve adding some structure to the process by setting deadlines, spending time on problems so that you outlast other participants, or overloading the system so that individuals are distracted with other problems, thus enabling you to make decisions. Finally, you can bring flexibility into the system by allowing individuals to act first on a problem and then analyze the outcome rather than trying to anticipate the outcome and limit options. Although this latter strategy can lead to chaos, it can also lead to creativity within the organization. Knowing when to take such risks is part of the learning process of becoming a manager.

In the bureaucratic environment, decisions are made by following the rules. If you want to change procedures or make changes in the department, you will need to begin by getting the group to agree to change the rules of the organization. Then you can introduce change into the unit. In participatory processes, you will usually find that many decisions are made by consensus. Here the individuals in the process agree that they can support the solution or decision even if it is not their favorite alternative or option.

As a manager using participatory processes, you are not limited to consensus building for making decisions. Other strategies can be effective depending on the type of problem to be resolved. For example, Vroom, in his work on decision making, notes that the context of the decision and the importance of the decision can lead to other strategies.[4] The less important the decision is to the participants, the more structured the problem, and the simpler the options, the more likely you can impose a solution or bargain a solution rather than have to come to a consensus. If a crisis situation exists and is accepted as such by participants, then imposing a solution may be very effective to resolve the crisis. In such cases, it is helpful to analyze the situation with the members of your department once the crisis is resolved to ensure that everyone understands what decision was made and why.

Another way to look at decision making in a participatory environment is provided by Plunkett and Fournier.[5] They identified four methods of decision making that can be effective in a participatory environment. Majority vote can be used when issues are relatively minor and the individuals in the department agree to go along with the majority decision. Unanimity is needed when everyone in the department must agree with the decision. Deciding department goals or values, for example, requires that everyone buy into and support the outcome. A third method that can be used in a participatory environment is that of imposing a decision. When the issue is relatively minor, you can likely declare a solution and move on to the next issue. Finally, the authors describe a process called "plop." Here someone gives a suggestion for how to resolve a problem, and the group simply goes along. The issue is resolved and the group can move on to more important agenda items.

MULTIPLE MODELS IN THE ORGANIZATION

In our complex organizations, a department chair is likely to find that a variety of decision-making models can be present simultaneously within the organization. For example, you may find that more rule-bound operations such as technical processing functions use more bureaucratic decision-making processes than other decision-making models. When working with colleagues in such an environment, you need to find out the rules that govern the processes before you try to make changes. Changing the rules will change the processes more easily than other forms of negotiation.

In branch systems, you may find that political bargaining behavior occurs more frequently if goals are not shared between the branches and the main library units, or if goals vary among the branches. Here being aware of the different value systems in place can help you choose strategies for negotiating common solutions to perceived problems.

Garbage can decision making can appear anywhere in a large organization where participants have the freedom to act independently. In the academic community, this type of behavior can be seen in faculty processes where faculty members can choose how they wish to spend their time and resources. Faculty and library professionals often share the characteristic of being able to set their own agendas and goals independent of the goals of the organization. In such situations, garbage can processes may easily occur. Recognizing and managing this chaotic behavior are a true challenge for today's manager.

When goals are shared and participants are committed to working together, you can develop an environment that encourages participatory decision making. Here shared power and commitment can make it possible to reach consensus among professionals about how to proceed and how to meet organizational and unit objectives.

SUCCESSFUL DECISION MAKING

You can improve your chances of making successful decisions by recognizing the different processes that are present in your organization and designing strategies that blend well with those processes.[6] You can manage the decision-making process. But to do that you need to resist the temptation to find a quick fix for problems, accept the uncertainty that is part of any decision-making process, and learn what strategies will work in your organizations and which ones will not work.

Decision making is a process you need to personally manage rather than delegate. Leaving issues to others and expecting them to develop successful solutions will not lead to success. Rather you need to search for understanding and be sure you have a clear idea of what issues you are trying to resolve. You need to look beyond the obvious symptoms of a given situation to see the bigger issue. A deeper understanding of the issues can lead you to opportunities and solutions that may not have been obvious when you first identified a problem.

Do set objectives or desired outcomes when looking at problems. Then look at a variety of ideas and opportunities to meet that outcome. Having a sense of the destination or the goal you wish to achieve will help guide the exploration of alternatives and provide more guidance for creative solutions. It is important in any decision-making process that you stress idea creation and solution generation to be sure that a number of aspects of a complex problem are identified and addressed. In addition, you will want to consider more than one option before choosing a course of action. By considering more than one option, you can develop more creative designs for problem solution and implementation of that solution.

You will also need to deal with barriers to action. Do ask what elements in the organization or the environment can block a successful implementation and then address these barriers in your plans. By considering what can prevent success before you begin implementation of a solution, you are more likely to be prepared to overcome problems as they arise in the implementation process.

By carefully considering the decision-making process, by practicing clear thinking in examining problems, and by promoting diplomatic actions in designing solutions, you will be more likely to have a successful decision-making process.

CONCLUSION

Decision making is a vital part of a manager's position. Yet, as is true of most management skills, one size or process does not fit all situations. As a manager, you need to understand the various ways that decisions can be made and then choose the strategy that is most effective for the given situation. By managing the decision-making process, and recognizing that each situation can be different, you will have a good chance of making good decisions that can resolve problems and lead to successful implementation of plans and actions.

NOTES

1. For a complete analysis of decision-making models, see: Joan Giesecke, "Making Decisions under Chaotic Conditions," Ph.D. diss., George Mason University (Ann Arbor, Mich.: University Microfilms, 1988).

2. Lee Bolman and Terrance Deal, *Modern Approaches to Understanding and Managing Organizations* (San Francisco: Jossey-Bass), 250.

3. Joan Giesecke, "Recognizing Multiple Decision-Making Models: A Guide for Managers," *College and Research Libraries* 54 (1993): 103-14.

4. Victor Vroom and Arthur Jago, *The New Leaders Managing Participation in Organizations* (Englewood Cliffs, N.J.: Prentice-Hall, 1988), 61.

5. Lorne C. Plunkett and Robert Fournier, *Participative Management: Implementing Empowerment* (New York: Wiley, 1991), 36-39.

6. Paul C. Nutt, "Surprising but True: Half the Decisions in Organizations Fail," *Executive Management* 13 (November 1999): 88-89.

8

Communication Skills

Communication, the "C" word of management. Some days it seems that no matter what the problem or issue may be, someone will inevitably say, "It's just a communication problem." It would seem that if we could only communicate better, all problems would disappear.

Communication is the true lifeline of the unit. It is how you stay connected to your unit and how your staff stays connected to you. The communication system can be very fragile, easily upset, or destroyed if you do not pay attention to how communication occurs in the unit and how individuals within the unit communicate with each other.

As a department head, you should already have good, basic communication skills. Numerous books, self-help tapes, videos, and articles are published regularly to help you improve basic writing, speaking, and listening skills. One of the first lessons a department head needs to learn is that while good communication skills are a must, not all problems will be solved simply through conversation. Problems can also be the result of such issues as differences in values, limited resources, or conflicting policies and procedures. To begin to address these complex problems, you need more than just good communication skills. You also need good conflict resolution, negotiation, mediation, and facilitation skills.

COMMUNICATION MODEL

Communication is described in a very basic model of sender, receiver, method of communication, and feedback. These four basic components describe all forms of communication (see figure 8.1).

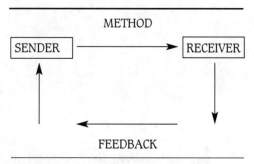

Figure 8.1   Communications Model

The sender is the person who begins the process. The individual has an idea or message he or she wishes to transmit to others. The sender may consciously decide which words to use to communicate the thought or idea. The sender may not realize that nonverbal cues are also a part of the transmission.

The sender chooses a method to use to communicate the message. The method for written communication can include a formal report, a memo, or an informal e-mail message. Verbal communication can include face-to-face conversation, a telephone call, or a group meeting. The medium selected can influence how a message is received. A formal report may seem to be more important than an informal e-mail. More care may be taken in how a memo on paper is written than how an e-mail message is constructed. A form letter may be ignored while a personally addressed letter may receive more attention. A face-to-face conversation may be more effective than an impersonal e-mail message. As a manager, it is important that you know how a particular medium will impact the receiver, know how different members of your unit prefer to receive information, and then try to match the medium with the message and the receiver.

The receiver is the person to whom the communication is addressed. The person for whom the message is intended may receive and understand the message, may choose to ignore the message, or may not understand the message. Being aware of potential barriers that can prevent communication and working to remove as many of the barriers as possible will increase the chances that the message will be received.

Feedback is the final essential element of the communication model. Feedback is the receiver's attempt to convey to the sender what message has been received. Feedback is critical as it helps the sender know if the message that was received is the message that he or she meant to send. Feedback includes both verbal and nonverbal clues. As a manager, you need to watch for feedback from your messages to assess the impact you are having.

One problem that can arise in the communication system is noise in the process. Noise is anything that can interfere with the clear transmission of the message. In written communication, noise can include bad grammar, poor spelling, or even poor formatting of the document. In verbal communication, noise can include sounds in the environment that make it difficult for one to hear the message, poor speaking skills, or even gestures such as putting your hand in front of your mouth.

As a manager you need to be very aware of your own communication skills and be sure that you are making every effort possible to improve your basic skills so that you communicate effectively with everyone in the organization.

CONFLICT RESOLUTION SKILLS

As a department head, you will also need to add to your skill set by learning and practicing good negotiation and conflict resolution skills. When you are effective in resolving conflicts, conflicts become a catalyst for creativity and change instead of a barrier to good group and interpersonal interactions.

What Is Conflict?

Conflict exists when there is a difference between two or more people that results in tension and mistrust. It can also be the result of disagreements about ideas or interests. When conflict arises, tension increases in the department and you are faced with needing to help the people resolve their differences. Unmanaged conflict can lead to communication breakdowns, increased emotional intensity, and possibly violence. Managed conflict can lead to problem resolution and creative change.

People approach conflict in a variety of ways. A very common approach is that of avoidance. Here the people do not deal with the conflict nor do they resolve it. They simply let the conflict remain as a source of tension in the unit.

Another approach may be confrontation. Here one person will put his/her own needs and interests above those of other members of the group. Resolution of the conflict may occur if the other party simply accedes to the wishes of the confronter.

A third approach is that of accommodation. Here a person ignores his/her own needs and interests and gives into the others involved in the conflict.

A fourth approach is that of compromise. In a compromise situation, each person in the conflict gets a part of what they want. There is a balance formed among the needs of the members of the group.

A fifth approach is that of collaboration. Here the people involved in the conflict work together to find a solution that satisfies everyone's needs.

Finally, in some circumstances, the members of the group may appeal to a higher authority for a ruling or resolution. This may occur when the group cannot come to a satisfactory solution but still wants to see the conflict resolved.

Perhaps the hardest thing for you, as a new department head or team leader, to learn is that you need to be skilled at each of these approaches and be able to use them as needed. Relying on only one style or approach will greatly limit your ability to manage different situations. For example, if two people are very close to the resolution of an issue, it may be helpful to compromise so that each person gets part of what they want. In other situations, it may be important to work toward a collaborative solution so that all members of the group feel that they have truly benefited from the solution.

Using Different Approaches

Learning when to use a particular conflict handling approach can be a challenge to new department heads who may be uncomfortable trying some of the approaches. The following section outlines how a manager can best use the different styles to resolve or decrease conflict.

AVOIDANCE

This style is best used when the issue is less important than other issues facing the organization or individuals. Some issues are so far off track or so unimportant to the overall objectives of the department that they are best avoided. This way the manager does not spend time, energy, and resources trying to resolve unimportant issues. Avoidance is also appropriate when the potential damage of confronting a situation is greater than the benefits that would come from resolving conflicts. Too, it may be appropriate to avoid a conflict situation until the individuals involved have time to cool down, reconsider the situation, and begin a constructive process of conflict resolution. Finally, avoidance is also appropriate when you need time to gather more information before beginning to consider possible solutions.

CONFRONTATION

Sometimes it is appropriate to confront an issue head on and take decisive action. This can be particularly true in emergency situations, in situations when an unpopular course of action needs to be implemented, or when the issue is vital to the group welfare and you are sure you have the right approach. As a style, confrontation should be used judiciously as it can lead to further problems, hurt feelings, and set up a cycle of victims and persecutors.

ACCOMMODATION

Accommodation is particularly appropriate when you realize you are wrong, to allow a better position to be heard, or to show that you can be reasonable. It is also a useful approach when the issue is more important to the other person than to you, or as a gesture of goodwill to maintain a cooperative relationship. It can be useful as a way to preserve harmony in the department or to help members of the department to learn and develop by trying new ideas and taking risks.

COMPROMISE

Compromise is a useful strategy when the issue is moderately important and each person in the conflict can reach part of his or her objectives. It can be useful as a way to temporarily resolve an issue or provide a quick solution so the department can move on to more important matters. It is also a good backup strategy when other styles such as collaboration or confrontation fail.

COLLABORATION

Collaboration allows for an integrated solution to important issues. It is often thought of as a "win-win" approach, where all participants in the process reach a solution that satisfies their needs. It allows the group to blend different perspectives, to gain commitment from group members, and to seek a consensus decision. It requires that the individuals involved work through hard feelings, consider all options, and work together to resolve the conflict.

ADVANCED COMMUNICATION SKILLS

One skill that is a key to successful conflict resolution is that of active listening. Active listening is more than just hearing what a person is saying. It is the process of trying to understand what the speaker means as well as what words are being said. Active listening involves:

1. *Sensing:* Using all of your senses to take in information.
2. *Interpreting:* Evaluating the meaning of the information.
3. *Checking:* Reflecting on what you have heard in an effort to gain a mutual understanding of the speaker's message.[1]

Sensing: The beginning of the listening process. Here you are not only listening to the speaker, but also observing nonverbal cues that help explain the message. The tone, volume, and rate of speech are also cues about the meaning of the message.

Interpreting: The process of evaluating what has been said and observed. Here you try to determine what the speaker intended to communicate.

Checking: One of the most important steps. Here you verify with the speaker that you have correctly heard the message, using a reflective statement such as "What I heard you say is" or "As I understand your point, it is."

Asking open-ended questions is an important part of practicing active listening. Follow-up questions such as "Could you say more about that issue?" will give the speaker an opportunity to expand on ideas and clarify his or her points. If a message is ambiguous, clarifying questions can help identify the issues. Questions such as "Could you provide an example of?" or "Could you tell us what you mean by?" can help a speaker focus his or her points and clarify the issues. Finally, probing questions can be used to be sure all information is shared. Questions such as "Any other ideas on this?" or simply "Anything else?" can be enough to get a group to look at other alternatives or bring up other issues.

These kinds of questions, along with active listening skills, help the department members communicate more effectively and share ideas in nonthreatening ways. Using effective active listening skills also helps members of the department feel that their concerns are being heard, that they are a part of the department's efforts, and that their contributions to the department are recognized and appreciated.

As a department chair, you will also want to be aware of the barriers to active listening so that you can be sure you are not taking listening for granted.[2]

The first barrier is trigger words. These are words that elicit an emotional response. Some words such as *thank you* or *please* create a positive feeling. Some words may create a negative feeling. As a department chair, you need to be aware of what words cause you to stop listening. What words cause you to react emotionally instead of objectively to the speaker?

The second barrier is that of interpretation. We may have a different meaning for a given word than that of the speaker. It is important as a manager to check to be sure that you are assigning the same meaning to a word as that of the speaker.

A third barrier is that of personal issues. Sometimes our personal lives interfere with our ability to focus and to listen. As a department chair, you need to be sure that problems in your personal life are not interfering with your ability to focus and to listen in your work life.

A fourth barrier is simply fatigue. When we are tired, it's harder to practice active listening skills. When you are tired, schedule more breaks for a group session and ask the group to help keep track of what is being said.

Finally, a fifth barrier to active listening skills is our own assumptions, prejudices, and beliefs. Our values and beliefs influence what we hear and how we interpret what is being said. As a manager, you need to be aware of your own beliefs and assumptions and be conscious of how those beliefs impact what you hear.

Active listening skills are part of the foundation of basic skills for a department chair or manager. With good listening skills you will be better able to negotiate with your staff, resolve conflicts, and work more effectively with your peers. Without good listening skills, you will miss much of what is being said and will be unable to effectively communicate within your organization.

CONCLUSION

While good communication skills helped you get your job as a department head, now you will want to add to your skill set. In addition to good basic oral and written skills, you will want to develop or enhance your active listening skills, conflict resolution skills, and negotiation skills. With this expanded toolbox of communication skills, you will be able to ensure that communication within your unit flows smoothly and that problems can be addressed successfully.

NOTES

1. Richard G. Weaver and John D. Farrell, *Managers as Facilitators* (San Francisco: Berrett-Koehler, 1997), 136.
2. Ibid., 139.

9

Structuring Your Department

From Bureaucracies to Teams

One decision you will want to consider as you make changes in your unit is how to structure the unit. In today's environment, there are still two major systems to consider when you think about restructuring or reorganizing your unit: bureaucratic structures or team-based structures.

How you structure your department or unit will be determined by what type of work your unit is doing. Some units in a library perform repetitive tasks while other units are more unstructured. For example, a technical processing unit may have more rules for the workflow than a public services unit that works directly with patrons. As a manager, you may find that you can develop a bureaucratic approach to a large technical processing unit while a public services unit needs a more fluid structure. Conversely, you may find that a team approach is effective regardless of the type of work that is being done. Your challenge as a manager is to find a structure that is effective for you and for the members of your unit.

For most of the twentieth century, organizations followed a traditional bureaucratic structure with a defined hierarchy, division of labor, and identified roles and responsibilities. A well-ordered bureaucracy was a good approach for large, complex organizations. The bureaucratic form brought order to chaos and provided a rational basis for structuring the work of the organization. Unfortunately, many large organizations added unnecessary layers and created inefficient structures, giving bureaucracies a bad reputation.

The dissatisfaction with the excesses of some bureaucratic forms has lead to a variety of management fads aimed at streamlining the organization. Whether moving to total quality management, reengineering, downsizing, rightsizing, or generally decreasing the size of the organization, the goal of the redesign was to increase efficiency and decrease waste. Such efforts have not proven to be overwhelmingly successful, and managers still struggle to find ways to structure the work to achieve organizational goals.

BUREAUCRACIES

Bureaucracies do not have to be inefficient. In the original theory of bureaucracies, Max Weber emphasized the following key elements:

1. Division of labor
2. Hierarchy of authority to coordinate activities
3. Career paths and career development opportunities for individual employees
4. Large organizations with stable structures and stable reporting lines
5. Objective personnel policies and procedures
6. Rule-based organizations[1]

These characteristics lead to a highly efficient, large organization where individuals know how jobs fit in with the overall organization. The organization revolves around positions and offices rather than individuals so that work can continue even as personnel change.

Bureaucracies work well when the main tasks for the units of the organization are routine or repetitive. In libraries, many technical operations and clerical operations fit this model. In these cases, a manager looks for continuous improvement to increase efficiency and decrease costs. In order to promote continuous improvement, managers need employees who are motivated to look for ways to improve operations. However, typical bureaucratic structures can lead to low motivation and lack of involvement in decision making by employees. The dilemma for management is how to have an efficient bureaucracy and motivated employees who will suggest improvements in operations.

Paul Adler, in his article "Building Better Bureaucracies," provides an answer for today's managers.[2] He notes that bureaucracies include both technical and social structures. Most of the work on bureaucracies has concentrated on technical structures, on how to organize the work for maximum efficiency and ignore the social structure of the unit. For Adler, managers can avoid the dilemma of how to create motivating bureaucracies by reviewing the social structure of the unit. A social structure that will result in motivated employees includes the following elements:

1. Emphasis on problem-solving skills
2. Adequate training so employees have the needed skills
3. Control shared between management and employees
4. Hierarchy based on expertise, not seniority
5. Participatory processes included
6. Mistakes viewed as learning opportunities

These basic elements can be a part of a bureaucratic structure. Employees can be involved in designing procedures, rules, and processes to increase efficiency. Employees can become a part of the problem-solving process. By involving employees in the creation of the technical structure of the organization, you can create a bureaucracy that is efficient and effective.

TEAMS

If the work you are managing is not routine or repetitive, you will want to look at different structures for the unit or organization. One of the more popular structures in today's environment is that of the team organization or group process oriented organization.

Work groups are created when a number of people are brought together to perform work or to achieve a common goal. Whether or not they develop into an efficient team depends on many factors. To distinguish working groups from teams, we need a definition of a team.

Jon Katzenbach and Douglas Smith define teams as "a small number of people with complementary skills who are committed to a common purpose, performance goals, and approach for which they hold themselves mutually accountable."[3]

Each element in this definition is important for creating high-performance teams. First, you need a small number of people so that team members can interact effectively, communicate easily, and convene easily. Next, the group must have the right mix of skills to accomplish the tasks of the unit. Technical, functional, problem-solving, and decision-making skills must all be present for the team to be able to accomplish its goals. The team members must also have a common purpose. The purpose should be broader than each individual's purpose and it should make team members feel important and excited about the team. Next, performance goals must relate directly to the group's purpose, or team members will be pulled in different directions. The goals should be realistic and challenging, calling for concrete work products that are important to team members. Fifth, team members must also agree on the approach the group takes to its work. The group has to agree to the internal work procedures and processes it will use to resolve issues, set priorities, and communicate. Finally the group must hold itself accountable for the accomplishment of goals and objectives. Unless the group takes responsibility for its own success, it will not become a true team.

If all of these elements are not present, you may have work groups or potential teams rather than teams. However, not every work group must become a team. Work groups can be effective when members interact primarily to share information and best practices, but do not have a common purpose or approach. In these cases, you may emphasize teamwork values of sharing and working together without having to create a true team.

Supervising Groups

Once you decide you will create a group- or team-oriented structure, you will need to adjust your supervisory style to match this organizational structure. The skills needed to supervise groups are different from those needed to supervise individuals. With groups, you need to understand both the formal and informal group structures. Peer pressure, informal group leaders, and group norms are powerful forces that can influence the behavior of group members.

To develop cohesive work units that are not necessarily teams, you will want to:

1. Understand the group's informal structure;
2. Be aware of what factors motivate group members, and attempt to create an environment that facilitates the satisfaction of those needs;
3. Give recognition and praise based on merit rather than seniority;
4. Have realistic expectations of employees and be sure those expectations are clear;
5. Take a sincere interest in the welfare of group members;
6. Develop group norms that center on cooperation;
7. Create a group identity by rotating job assignments and providing cross-training;
8. Help resolve problems with other parts of the organization;
9. Help create a positive attitude toward the unit.

These guidelines reflect basic good management practice for today's environment. Once you become comfortable letting go of the command and control approach to management, you can create working groups that are effective as easily as you can create a bureaucratic structure that is efficient and effective.

Team Leaders

Middle managers in a team-oriented structure may find that they are serving as team leaders rather than as traditional managers. The roles for team leaders are the same as the roles for today's department chair or middle manager. Team leaders serve as facilitators for the team, act as catalysts, and provide working leadership for the group. A good team leader helps keep the purpose of the team, the goals, and the approach relevant and meaningful. As a team leader, you help clarify the mission for the team and help the team stay focused on the goals. You also help build confidence and commitment for the individual members of the team. You will want to provide positive feedback for the group and avoid intimidation or coercive tactics.

As team leader, you also bring skills to the team. Facilitation skills will be crucial for you, as will good communication skills, good interpersonal skills, and good management skills. You will also need to be adept at managing the relationship between the team and the rest of the organization. You job is to remove obstacles for team members so that the team can accomplish its goals. Finally, team leaders are working leaders, carrying out the work of the team as they provide overall focus and leadership.

FLEXIBLE ALTERNATIVES

While the continuum from bureaucracies to teams describes how most departments are structured, new work relationships are adding new structures to our organization. One such change that you may face is the interest in contracting out part of a unit's work. Using contractors to carry out part of the ongoing activities of the department brings new challenges to middle managers. Instead of directly supervising front-line employees, you are now managing a contract for that work. Numerous articles and books can help you as you begin working with contractors. From a management viewpoint, part of your challenge will be to design a structure where contractors play a role in your unit, are accepted as part of the unit, and adapt or respond to the values, goals, and objectives of the unit. With contractors, you manage results, not time. This means you need to specify the outcomes or results you want from the work, rather than outlining procedures on how people will spend their time. It will be up to the contractor to determine how to get the work done to meet agreed-upon results for an agreed-upon fee.

A second change you may encounter is that of designing structures that include telecommuters. Not all of your employees may be on-site. Some may work from home and some may have offices elsewhere and interact mostly through e-mail. Your challenge is to design systems that make these employees feel a part of the unit. You will need structures that keep nonwork-site employees informed about changes in the departments, new policies and procedures, and plans and objectives. You will need ways to monitor work to ensure that all employees are treated fairly. You will also need to keep track of changing personnel issues, policies, or laws that impact telecommuters and other off-site employees.

A third group you may have in your department is part-time employees and those who are only hired for a particular project. While libraries have relied heavily on student employees to cover tasks such as shelving materials, organizations are finding that some permanent staff are interested in part-time work and more flexible schedules than traditional full-time employees have had. Your challenge is to find ways to keep these people engaged in the organization and not treat them as transient employees. These people are important to the unit and need to feel respected and accepted as a part of the unit.

The departmental structure of a core group of professionals, contract employees, telecommuters, and part-time employees has been described as a shamrock, with each employee group representing a leaf of the shamrock.[4] While the structure is quite logical, it is not necessarily easy to run.

Each group needs to be managed differently, yet each group has to fit into the whole. Policies may vary among the groups, and meetings of the whole department may be difficult if not impossible to schedule. Here is a place where clear communication and established communication structures are essential. Keeping everyone informed about department activities, policies, and procedures as well as about activities, objectives, and goals can go a long way toward creating a whole department out of separate structures.

CONCLUSION

The organizational structure for the unit should help facilitate rather than hinder the work of the unit. Organizational structures can vary from traditional bureaucratic designs to the more fluid team-oriented structures. Your task is to match structure to work processes. If the organizational structure for the unit is in conflict with the social structure of the unit, you will not have an effective unit. If the organizational structure does not mesh well with the workflow of the unit, then the members of the unit will find ways to work around the structure. This inevitably leads to inefficiencies and waste. When the organizational structure matches the work of the unit, you will have an effective structure that can help your unit achieve success.

NOTES

1. Harold Gortner, *Administration in the Public Sector* (New York: Wiley, 1981), 100-102.

2. Paul Adler, "Building Better Bureaucracies," *Academy of Management Executive* 13 (November 1999): 36-47.

3. Jon R. Katzenbach and Douglas K. Smith, *The Wisdom of Teams: Creating the High Performance Organization* (Cambridge, Mass.: Harvard Business School Press, 1993), 45.

4. Charles Handy, *The Age of Unreason* (Cambridge, Mass.: Harvard Business School Press), 87-115.

10

Putting It All Together

By now you may be wondering why anyone would want to be a middle manager, department head, or team leader. Why take a position where you have little or no control over the work of the unit and the actions of the members of the unit, but are responsible for the unit's success? While today's middle managers are not in positions to command others to act, these people are vital members of the management team for the organization. Through negotiation and collaboration, today's middle managers can and do provide leadership to the organization. They can take the initiative to create new programs, take risks to bring about change, and provide needed support to the members of the unit. Whether you are managing professionals, managing other managers, or managing staff positions, you can bring creativity and innovation to the organization. You can be the difference between a successful organization that meets its service goals and an unsuccessful organization that barely survives. You do not need to abdicate leadership to the upper levels of management. You can provide leadership in the middle.

BEGINNING AGAIN

As outlined throughout this book, how you begin your position will set the tone for how you interact with the members of your unit. If you make too many changes before you really understand the department, you will have a difficult time establishing a good working relationship with your staff. If you take too long to make decisions, you will be seen as indecisive and ineffectual. Your goal is to develop a balance between action and inaction, and between change and the status quo.

You can improve your chances of success as a new manager by recognizing that you need to learn everything you can about the organization rather than assuming, based on previous experiences, that you already know how the members of your department work and act. You need to let go of the idea that you are the expert, and realize that as a new person you are responsible for learning about the organization and its culture. While your previous experience and expertise can help you in your assessment of the organization, you must remind yourself to keep an open mind while you are learning about the organization.

Initial Steps to Survival

To survive your first year on the job and be successful, you will want to create and follow your own checklist of the tasks you need to complete. These include the following:

1. Before you begin your new position, learn as much as you can about the organization and the unit.

2. Design a set of questions to help you obtain the information you need to learn about your unit and about the members of your staff.

3. Meet with every member of your unit, your boss, and your peers, to learn about them, their areas of responsibility, their concerns, and their ideas about your department. You will gain valuable insights by seeing how others view your department.

4. Make some initial changes as you identify those problems that can be easily resolved. You need to show some initiative in your first few months to help the members of your unit and others in the organization see you as a leader.

5. Help the unit review or redesign its vision, mission, goals, and objectives. Be sure you are setting a direction that matches that of the

organization, is realistic for the unit, and provides challenges and opportunities for growth for the members of the department. Use your planning skills to help the unit set directions and set goals.

6. Participate in the work of the unit. Show that you understand what each member of the unit does and that you understand the workflow of the unit. Practice interactive delegation, balancing telling people what to do with helping them design their own implementation strategies.

7. Build good working relationships with your peers and your boss. You are responsible for ensuring that your department interacts successfully with other units in the organization. You are also responsible for developing a good working relationship with your boss. You need to adjust your style to match that of your boss so that you develop a trusting relationship. Managing up the organization is as important as managing within your department and managing across departments.

By the end of your first year, then, you should have a good working knowledge of the organization and an understanding of how your unit fits in with other sections of the organization. You will have developed an initial set of goals and objectives with the department and have begun to make needed changes. You should have a good beginning knowledge of the strengths and weaknesses of the members of your department and be starting to think of how you can help your department members grow and progress as professionals.

Next Steps

Once you have a basic understanding of the organization and the department, you can begin making larger changes that may be needed to help your department grow and succeed in a changing environment. You may need to restructure parts of the unit or it may be time to think about changing the overall structure. Do you need a team environment? Do you need a more effective bureaucratic approach? Do you need some combination of different types of structures? These decisions should be made in discussion with the members of the department as you look at how best to organize the work of the unit to achieve its goals.

As you develop organizational structures that will meet the needs of the unit, you will want to be working on helping the members of your unit develop career plans and career development opportunities. Mentoring skills will be essential here as you want to help your department members assess their own strengths and try to design positions that will emphasize and use those strengths. While concentrating on weaknesses has been the traditional focus of evaluation and development plans, you will be more successful if you can concentrate on a person's strengths and how to develop those strengths while helping the person learn ways to compensate for areas that are not as strong. This change in focus from weaknesses to strengths will give you a more positive approach as you work with the members of your units.

You will also need to pay attention to your own career development. Learn about your own strengths and weaknesses. Design a development plan that helps you get training in areas where you want to learn new skills or improve existing skills. Look for opportunities that are challenging for you so that you too can grow as a professional as you are helping others in your unit develop and grow. Taking care of your own career will help send a signal to the members of your unit that you do care about development and growth. However, if you concentrate on your own needs at the expense of others, you will not be viewed as supportive of the unit. Be sure you balance opportunities for yourself with opportunities for the members of the unit so that everyone benefits.

By the second year, you will have addressed many of the technical or workflow issues, and begun to work on the social interactions within the department and between the department and the rest of the organization. Your department should have a sense of action, and of positive changes that are making the unit more effective. You will be working to help ensure that every member of your unit has the opportunity to be successful in his or her own position.

SKILLS REVIEW

What skills will you need to accomplish the changes you need to make as a middle manager? You need good negotiation and communication skills. Your role is as much that of a diplomat as of a manager. You will be a leader, a facilitator, and a catalyst for action. You will not be able to simply issue orders and commands and expect them to be carried out. Rather, you will be negotiating what needs to happen in the department and how tasks will be accomplished.

Besides good negotiation skills, you need good technical management skills. These include planning skills, decision-making skills, and resource management skills. You also need to be aware of the many legal issues that are part of today's organizations. You will want to have a good understanding of basic legal requirements of affirmative action and equal opportunity rules, know about the Americans with Disabilities Act and its impact on the workplace, and understand changes in personnel laws and court cases that will impact what you can do.

Finally, you will want to learn about new organizational structures and organizational designs that can help you improve the effectiveness of your unit. You will want to stay abreast of the various management theories and how these may impact or help you accomplish your goals. You will want to know the difference between a total quality management or continuous improvement program and a learning organization effort. You will want to review the differences between bureaucratic approaches and team approaches. You will want to find and use those management ideas that fit with the culture and design of your department and that help make the unit successful.

LEADING FROM THE MIDDLE

Being a middle manager, department head, or team leader can be an exciting and challenging position. While you may feel squeezed between upper management, who can make decisions that impact your unit, and the members of your department, who may or may not want to move in the directions you want to set, you can provide leadership to the organization. You can help set the direction for your department, move the unit forward, and create an innovative and exciting department. You can succeed in middle management by remembering that this level of the organization is one of building partnerships and collaborative relationships. By working to integrate your department into the organization and build bridges to other departments, you can create a vital, dynamic, exciting unit that helps the organization reach its goals while providing growth opportunities and challenges to the members of the unit. As a manager, your success will be evident in the development of successful professionals and staff members who are committed to the success of the department and the success of the organization. You will succeed when they succeed. Your rewards will come from helping others while showing that you understand how to provide working leadership for the organization.

Index

Joan Giesecke is the Dean of Libraries, University of Nebraska–Lincoln Libraries. She has received a doctorate in public administration from George Mason University, an MLS from the University of Maryland, a master's degree in management from Central Michigan University, and a BA in economics from SUNY at Buffalo. She has worked in special, public, and academic libraries in a variety of management positions. Her research interests include organizational decision making and management skills. She is a former editor of *Library Administration & Management*, editor of *Practical Help for New Supervisors*, editor of *Scenario Planning for Libraries*, and has published numerous articles on management issues.